How to work with Young People

Manual for youth leaders

Ken Anderson
Geraldine Anderson
Craig Mitchell

Uniting Church Press
Melbourne

Published by
THE JOINT BOARD OF CHRISTIAN EDUCATION
65 Oxford Street, Collingwood 3066 Australia

HOW TO WORK WITH YOUNG PEOPLE

National Library of Australia
Cataloguing-in-Publication entry.

Anderson, Ken.
    How to work with young people
    Bibliography.
    ISBN 0 85819 801 0.
    1. Christian life – Study and teaching. 2. Church work with youth – Uniting Church in Australia. I. Anderson, Geraldine, 1961–   . II. Mitchell, Craig, 1957–   . III. Title.

248.48793

First printed 1991
Reprinted 1992, 1994, 1997

Design by Kelvin Young
Illustrated by Bronwyn Halls
Typeset in Bitstream Swiss by JBCE on Ventura Publisher
Printed by Openbook Publishers
JB94/3544

Contents

		page
Introduction		**5**
Chapter 1	**What is youth ministry?**	**7**
Chapter 2	**Participation in the church**	**23**
Chapter 3	**Recruiting leaders**	**35**
Chapter 4	**Leadership development**	**43**
Chapter 5	**Making groups work**	**57**
Chapter 6	**Communicating and caring**	**75**
Chapter 7	**Program planning**	**87**
Chapter 8	**Discipleship groups**	**113**
Chapter 9	**Worship and devotions**	**123**
Chapter 10	**Small church groups**	**141**
Chapter 11	**Evangelism**	**153**
Chapter 12	**Social issues**	**163**
Chapter 13	**Camping**	**175**
Recommended reading		**200**

INTRODUCTION

YOUTH MINISTRY – A CONVERSATION...

'But I thought the object of youth ministry was to get more kids into the church, you know, put bottoms on pews.'

'That's crazy, where in the Bible does it say that God wants us to sit people (especially young people) on seats?'

'Well what's this manual about then? Doesn't it tell me how to fill up my church, make more people come?'

'Hopefully this manual will give you the know-how to begin helping to change young peoples' lives. Change their lives with the good news of the gospel.'

'Is that the bottom line?'

'This manual is more than just a 'how to do it' book. It says a lot about why we do things, helps us get priorities right.'

'Will it mean more kids will come to my group?'

'Read it, learn from it, catch the vision of it. Then ask yourself that question.'

This Manual for Youth Leaders is the reflection of many years of experimenting, trying new ideas and building on old foundations by a range of people from around Australia working in an area where there are few experts but many practitioners.

Dino Anderson and Craig Mitchell have worked closely with me in a 'think tank' and on the script. The manual however reflects and contains the work of many including Graham Johnson, Bruce Mullan, Warren Smith, Steve Francis, Fuzz Kitto, Ian O'Reilly, Grant Nichol, Heather McMinn, John Mallison, John U'Ren, George Davies, Leigh Pope, Pat Baker, and the training courses developed and conducted around Australia.

Behind each of the above names have been a number of mentors who have encouraged us to dream our dreams and see our visions – to match these with direction from God's Spirit and then 'to go for them'.

David Merritt and the Joint Board of Christian Education have been the stable and supporting foundation of Youth Ministry in the Uniting Church through the Eighties.

Here's to the Nineties.

Ken Anderson
January 1990

Chapter 1

What is youth ministry?

What is youth ministry? The big picture

But what is youth ministry really?   9

What are young people like?   10

What do young people like to do?   11

What are the keys to effective ministry with
young people?   13

How can we encourage our church to set goals,
develop and evaluate its youth ministry?   16

WORKSHEET 1: What is your church doing in
youth ministry?   19

WORKSHEET 2: Questions to young people   20

WORKSHEET 3: Pastoral care of young people   21

WORKSHEET 4: Lettergram   22

But what is youth ministry really?

When we ask, 'What is the purpose of youth ministry in the church?', we need to ask firstly what is the purpose of the church. As we understand the purpose of the church we will then know what needs to be aimed for in youth ministry. As an example we have taken the statement on purposes from the Uniting Church's Constitution and explored what it means for youth ministry.[1]

The purposes of the church are to:	Implications for youth ministry
• provide for the worship of God	worship
• proclaim the gospel of the Lord Jesus Christ	evangelism
• promote Christian fellowship	community and friendship building ecumenical involvement
• nurture believers in the Christian faith	Christian education
• engage in mission	outreach social justice
• assist in human development and toward the improvement of human relationships	personal growth youth participation in the church
• meet human need through charitable and other services	service
• do other such things as may be required in obedience to the Holy Spirit	anything else as the Spirit moves

1 See *Constitution and Regulations* of the Uniting Church in Australia. Uniting Church Press, Melbourne, 1990.

What are some examples?

See WORKSHEET 1 for suggestions, in the categories above, that are appropriate for youth ministry. Please note:

Every congregation should be providing opportunities for and with young people in all of the above areas, taking into account the different needs of different age groups.

But – it is not necessary or usually possible for one youth group or activity to attempt to cover all the areas.

There are a wide variety of forms in which youth ministry can take place.

For example:
Sunday school; youth group; young people on parish/congregational decision making bodies; Bible study groups; teaching Sunday school; service projects; outreach projects; social justice forums; religious education in schools; coffee shops; youth services; Sunday morning worship; singing groups; leadership training; involvement with community groups; being stewards; all age activities; crisis accommodation; family camps; small groups; job creation schemes; after school programs; holiday programs; social activities; etc.

Oversight of youth ministry in the Uniting Church is the responsibility of the Council of Elders. One way they can ensure this happens is by setting up a youth ministry Committee or Task Group.

What are young people like?

Young people vary like any group in society. Therefore to give a picture of an average young person would be irresponsible as each young person is an individual with particular likes, dislikes and characteristics.

This is important to keep in mind when dealing with young people. It is important not to lump them all into one group like zoo animals or marbles.

However, there are some common characteristics of young people that are true for many.

Young people are:

- Developing physically
- Developing mentally
  - learning
  - beginning to form values
  - beginning to question society
- Developing socially
  - being popular and having friends is important
- Developing significant relationships
  - between boys and girls
  - same sex relationships
- Developing an awareness of the world
  - caring about issues that affect them and the world, like environment, peace, injustice.

What do you think young people are like? Use WORKSHEET 2 'Questions to Young People'. Fill it out for yourself, then have some young people fill it out. Compare your answers.

When trying to work out what young people are like, it is best to ask them. This is what they say of themselves:

'We're GREAT'
'We're making lots of decisions'
'We're having lots of hassles'
'We need to go out with our own group a lot'
'We're fun and enthusiastic'
'We're under lots of pressure'
'Lots of us are involved in boy/girl relationships'
'Peer group pressure bothers and affects us'
'There are lots of changes in our lives'
'We are maturing and growing up'

Below are some basic needs of young people. You may find them helpful in your search to understand what young people are like.

Basic needs of young people

1. To achieve self acceptance

- Accepting your body.
- Understanding how your body changes through adolescence.
- Accepting your own sex and discovering what it means to be a boy or girl. Discovering and evaluating society's expectation of the male/female role.
- Feeling good about yourself.
- Knowing yourself (answering the question 'Who am I?')

2. To achieve emotional independence

- Becoming free of childlike dependence upon parents or other adults.
- Learning to make your own decisions and organise your own life.
- Developing a mature affection for parents and other adults.

3. To develop happy and relaxed relationships

- Meeting and keeping friends of both sexes and a variety of ages.
- Developing skills in the areas of inviting, refusing, resolving conflicts, and evaluating experiences.
- Experiencing loving and being loved.
- Discovering the privileges and responsibilities associated with belonging to a family, clubs, peer and community groups.
- Learning to distinguish between infatuation and more lasting forms of love.
- Preparing for marriage through dating, going steady, becoming deeply involved with a loved one.
- Facing the implications of settling down and establishing a home.

4. To develop a philosophy of life

- Selecting satisfying and socially acceptable ideals and standards (values and ethical controls).
- Interpreting the meaning and value of life.
- Exploring and understanding the religious dimension of experience.
- Evaluating the goals society offers and coping with the pressures of advertising and competing life styles.

5. To develop a satisfying vocational role

- Completing one's education.
- Seeking advice regarding possible vocations.

- Defining and developing priorities and interests.
- Seeking job satisfaction.

6. **To develop responsibility for what happens in the society and in the world**
   - Becoming involved in causes that are greater than self.

- Gaining the ability to communicate as a citizen in a democracy.
- Developing concepts of law, government, economics, politics and social organisation.

What do young people like to do?

Young people like to be with people their own age. It is helpful to divide them into small age-range groups to cater more fully for their differing needs. Young people between the ages of 12 and 14 will want and need different things from young people who are 16 or 17. Therefore some helpful age brackets are:

12-14/15 year olds
15-17/20 year olds
20 + year olds

In this manual, young people 15 years of age have been included in two age brackets. They can have their needs catered for in either of the age groups. They are in the middle, between the young adolescents who are exploring the change from being children to young people, and young adults who have moved beyond the initial changes of adolescence to more complicated issues of relationships, future career and lifestyle choices. Where each 15 year old will best be catered for will depend largely on the young person as an individual and the style of group offered by your church.

What do these young people, in these age groups, like to do? The Joint Board of Christian Education has done research into the area of 12-14 year olds and 15-17/20 year olds in the church, surveying young people in youth groups.

Here are some of the findings.

12-14/15 YEAR OLDS

This is the younger youth age bracket, and pre-adolescent stage for some young people.

Their interests and needs:

The interests of 12-14/15 year olds are wide-ranging and varied, but they indicate a clear preference for informal sports and social activities, together with hobbies and creative or cultural pursuits. A number of questions were asked about activities young people enjoy, like, or choose for themselves or for their church youth groups. These are summarised below.

To indicate the broadness of the range of interests 12-14/15 year olds have, as well as to help those who are planning for groups of 12-14/15 year olds, every activity mentioned by the young people has been included in the listing.

1. Team Sports (those requiring more than two people): football, soccer, netball, cricket, basketball, volleyball, softball, downball, field hockey, ice hockey, 'sport'.

2. Individual sports: roller skating, ice skating, tennis, squash, badminton, bowling, table tennis, gymnastics, athletics, trampoline, golf, darts, skateboarding, skiing, billiards, martial arts, archery, shooting, pinballs, slot cars, slot machines, grass skiing, calisthenics, hang gliding.

(Note: In this category, the answers include what 12-14/15 year olds themselves described as individual sports.)

3. Water activities: swimming, fishing, water skiing, surfing, sailing, canoeing, kayaking, skin diving, rowing, sun baking, water polo, water sports.

4. Bush activities: camping, hiking, nature study, nature crafts, cooking out, bird watching, ferreting, bush walking, rock climbing, caving, orienteering.

5. Other outdoor activities: picnics, barbecues, gardening, bike riding, horse riding, running, jogging, kite flying, mini bikes, walking, billy carts.

6. Creative/cultural activities: playing piano or other instruments (guitar, recorder, flute, drums), art, craft, being in musicals, singing, ballet, drama, graphics, writing poetry, dancing (disco, bush, ballroom, punk), painting, jazz ballet, writing songs, creative dance, sewing, films.

7. Social or group activities: talking to friends, being with friends, meeting new people, parties, playing games, eating, cooking, playing cards, having fun, hanging around, camps, trips, outings, meeting with other groups, discussions, fun things, discussing personal problems, mucking around, being with opposite sex, simulation games, hunts/chases, being with older kids, clubs, sleep overs, coffee shop.

8. Domestic activities: shopping, baby sitting, being with family, being with adults.

9. Individual or personal activities: reading, sleeping, thinking, learning about self, learning about life, playing with dog, playing with train, playing with electrical gear, learning to drive.

10. Study or school related activities: school, maths, science, study.

11. Specifically church related activities: club, Bible study, church worship, Sunday school, service projects, helping others, visiting elderly, outreach, devotions, prayers, fund raising, study electives, communication about program.

12. Entertainment: listening to pop music (radio, records, tapes), watching television.

Of the activities listed, the clear favourites for individuals and/or groups were (in order of preference):
1. skating
2. camps
3. trips and outings
4. swimming
5. active games
6. being with friends
7. dancing
8. bike riding.

Those activities liked least by all were:
1. writing songs
2. gardening
3. nature study
4. jazz ballet
5. martial arts
6. singing.

Most of the young people's favourite activities were clearly social and active. While it is possible to skate, ride a bike or swim alone, it is far more likely that this age group prefers to follow these activities with a group, or at least with one other person.

15-17/20 YEAR OLDS

This age group is a high pressured age group. Often they are in their final years at school and are encountering pressures from varying areas of their lives.

This age group likes:
discussion
prayer
games and fun
trips and outings
Bible study
refreshments
camps
singing
talks and lectures
sport
socials, parties
concerts/musicals/dramas/acting
roller skating/bowling/films
youth services/Presbytery run worship/ Synod youth services
fun, creative activities
devotions
bowling and skating
films
dances
drama
just being together.

Other activities not enjoyed were:
devotions
singing
doing nothing.

The activities 15-17 year olds wanted more of were:
camps
outings/trips
meeting other youth groups
discussion on life issues.

The activities they wanted less of were:
sport nights
games
boring studies.

The activities they wanted to add to the program which were not already there were:
meeting other youth groups
concerts
hikes (bike/back packing/walking)
inexpensive nights
discussions
outings
camps.

To 15-17 year olds, the ideal youth group program would be:
'An even balance of fun, exciting games, interesting program, devotions and supper'
'Discussion, games, supper and free time to talk'
'Anything energetic and fun, we need a release'

'The programs we have now are pretty good except for people who won't get involved and deliberately spoil them'
'The program has to be lively and energetic'.

20+ OR YOUNG ADULTS

This age group is often past the youth group experience and looking for other forms of social outlets.

Young adults are:
making career choices
making relationship and family choices
— marriage
— children
— singleness
mobile – they are often moving, leaving home, changing their environment
searching for more long term relationships and places in society
earning significant incomes and making choices about what they do with their money and resources.

Young adults either take their religion more seriously or they move away from the church altogether. According to the report on youth in the church from the *Combined Churches Survey for Faith and Mission*, 18-25 year olds are making significant choices about most things in their lives, especially the church. This age group has the mobility and the motivation to move away from churches and groups that do not suit them and either shop around for something else in that line or discontinue attendance altogether.

What are the keys to effective ministry with young people?

This rationale is a statement about an effective way for ministry with young people to run in a congregation or parish. It contains five key statements. Each of these is followed by:
a brief explanation of the key statement
a list of tasks
space for response.

The rationale, by providing space for response becomes a planning tool for those involved in youth ministry and a basis for the Council of Elders to prepare job descriptions for volunteer youth leaders. As such the rationale should be responded to annually. The aim is:
to affirm the importance of youth ministry
to assist the selection of suitable leaders
to assist leaders in their planning
to use fully leaders' skills and talents
to avoid unnecessary duplication
to encourage co-operation between groups by sharing of ideas and resources
to detect gaps in youth ministry.

KEY STATEMENT ONE

Youth ministry is based on the gospel.

The gospel is the good news that, in Jesus, the separation between God and men and women and between individuals is overcome. It is a message of reconciliation.

Yet it is more than a message It is the challenge to accept in faith what God has done. Such faith requires the commitment to grow in understanding and live in the positive relationship with God and others.

The great gospel themes of the love of God, the basic goodness of life, the reality of the conflict between good and evil, the worth of the individual, the importance of forgiveness and the reality of God's presence among us must be reflected in youth ministry.

TASKS

1.1 Provide opportunity to study the Bible to increase understanding of it.

1.2 Develop ways in which young people may be confronted by the gospel message.

1.3 Provide opportunity for the corporate worship of God and for participation in the sacraments. This should include opportunities for leadership.

1.4 Provide a forum for discussion and assistance for individuals so that each person may be encouraged and helped to develop personal patterns of prayer and Christian reading.

1.5 Maintain an openness for creative contact with non church young people. Maintain a willingness to present the challenge of the gospel in a non judgmental way which reflects the love of God.

KEY STATEMENT TWO

Youth ministry in the church finds its direction in the nature and purpose of the church.

Youth ministry is one facet of the ministry of the church; by its people to each other, and those beyond the church, under the grace of God. It cannot be separated from the unifying experiences of the community of faith; the worship of God, the preaching of the Word, the Sacraments of Baptism and Holy Communion, and the ministry of servanthood.

Because youth ministry is a facet of ministry oriented to young people it will be shaped by the gospel, and by the interests and needs of young people.

Thus, youth ministry must be by – and for young people. They must not be seen as, or allowed to become, passive attenders, followers, or apprentices. Many must play a significant part in planning and leadership among their peers and within the total ministry of the church.

TASKS

2.1 Develop within the parish the concept that youth ministry is part of the total ministry of the parish and that as such it takes place within a variety of settings, not all of which are single age group activities.

2.2 Ensure young people understand the meaning of, and are challenged to accept, the privileges and responsibilities of membership of the church.

2.3 Challenge young people to commit themselves to a

realistically planned giving of their time, gifts and money to support the mission of the church.

2.4 Expand the vision of young people in regard to the nature and diversity of the mission of the church in Australia within the community, and at the national and international levels. Challenge young people to be involved in this mission and support them in their efforts.

KEY STATEMENT THREE

Youth ministry is concerned with individuality and personal growth.

3.1 Provide opportunities for individuals to develop a healthy, realistic acceptance of self. This will include encouraging young people to participate in leadership and decision making and take on other responsibilities as appropriate to their skills and development.

3.2 Provide a forum and other experiences which enable young people to explore issues which are of concern to themselves. These will include:
personal identity, values, independence, empowerment, vocation, sexual development, education,

unemployment, AIDS, equality and inequality.

3.3 Provide opportunities for young people to relate with persons of both sexes in a relaxed, Christian environment. Care should be taken to provide activities appropriate to particular age groups.

3.4 Provide opportunity for reflection on positive and negative behaviour patterns and assistance to develop meaningful, healthy relationships with God and with members of both sexes.

3.5 Explore concepts and patterns of positive Christian citizenship and care of the environment.

....
....
....
....
....

KEY STATEMENT FOUR

Youth ministry in the Uniting Church is accountable to young people and to the Uniting Church in Australia.

Within the Uniting Church in Australia oversight of youth ministry is the responsibility of the Council of Elders. Presbytery and Synod also have a responsibility to provide support and encourage development of youth ministry.

All structures must remain the servant of the gospel, and of the people that are commissioned to serve. So accountability is a two way thing:

* young people are called to hear and respond to the gospel, and to play their part as full, responsible members of the Uniting Church.
* the Council of Elders, Presbytery and Synod agencies must demonstrate responsible care and interest and understanding towards young people as they fulfil their responsibilities within the church structure.

TASKS

4.1 Involve young people in leadership.

4.2 Develop ways to creatively use the candour, idealism, innovation, critical evaluation of young people in the life of the church.

4.3 Develop an effective consultative process so that young people may be informed of, and have input into, the activities of the parish.

4.4 Wherever possible, involve young people in decision making in the parish, particularly in regard to decisions that affect them.

4.5 Produce leader job descriptions which include the expectations of the Council of Elders, with clear description of the job to be done, anticipated time required, support to be offered, and any other requirements.

4.6 Develop a leader support system.

....
....
....
....
....

KEY STATEMENT FIVE

Youth ministry in the church is uniquely Australian in character.

As the call to faith is people rather than program centred and the gospel itself emphasises restored relationships, the context in which the good news is proclaimed and lived cannot be ignored. Thus it is a disservice to youth ministry to uncritically adopt patterns, structures and programs which have their origins in other countries. We are Australian and therefore have a different history and different needs and concerns and concepts, although we share the same gospel with youth ministry around the world.

There is need for the development of youth ministry that is distinctively Australian in character and which takes note of our multicultural environment.

5.1 Leaders should wherever possible draw on Australian images when planning programs and events so that young people are led to a greater appreciation of cultural heritage, can express the faith in typically Australian concepts, and can evaluate various aspects of Australian life. This will require that thought be given to the following aspects of life: isolation, the Aussie battler, the long week end, living in the Pacific Basin, unemployment, multiculturalism, betting, boozing, footy, suburbia, the country to city drift, rural decline, the dead heart, first world wealth, Australian art, music, writing and drama.

....

....

....

....

....

How can we encourage our church to set goals, develop and evaluate its youth ministry?

Youth ministry has to be a part of the church's ministry, not a separate appendage to the church, run by some concerned parents or young adults. Below are some useful exercises to do with the councils responsible for youth ministry in the church. In the Uniting Church it will be the Council of Elders.

The Uniting Church in Australia in its policy statement *Young People and Your Church* states the following about care and support for young people:

The elders and the minister should plan for the pastoral care of young people at least as thoroughly as for adults, ensuring that

• every young person is cared for by an elder who should talk with him or her at least 3 or 4 times each year
• the minister and elders give special attention to contacts with young people not in any group
• every youth group has an elder responsible for visiting it

regularly to share concerns of the Council of Elders and to listen to the views of young people
• suitable leaders are appointed to or recognised for all youth groups and briefed so that they understand the importance of pastoral care of young people
• the minister visits youth groups regularly, e.g. monthly, to get to know young people and to support young people and leaders.

The Council of Elders

How does it care for young people in the church and how does it support youth ministry?

Divide the leaders into small groups of 4 or 5 (maximum) people.

Hand out WORKSHEET 3, 'Pastoral Care of Young People' and WORKSHEET 4 'Lettergram'.

Ask elders to give their church a mark out of 10 for every point listed on the Pastoral Care sheet (1 is the lowest score, 10 is the

highest), then share their marks within their small groups.

The small groups should then discuss what they consider to be the strengths and weaknesses of the pastoral care of young people that is provided in their church. Note that the aim of the discussion is to discover ways to improve pastoral care, not to make people feel bad about things they aren't doing well.

Next ask each elder individually to write on WORKSHEET 4 a telegram to the Council of Elders saying what specific action they believe the Council of Elders should take with regard to pastoral care of young people. Ask elders to share their telegrams in their small groups, and see if there are any common suggestions for action.

Ask each group to report to the whole group what their most common action suggestions were. Write these suggestions on newsprint or a blackboard for everyone to see. If more than one group makes the same suggestion, put a tick next to it. Establish which action suggestions have the most support by telling the elders they have 3 votes each. Then go through each action suggestion in turn and ask for a show of hands as to who wishes to vote for it. Count and record the votes.

Of the action suggestions that have the most support, decide which you will carry out.

Decide how you will carry out each of the action suggestions chosen.

— Do some of the action on the spot.
— Refer specific actions to the people responsible for them.
— Set up a small short-term task group to bring recommendations to the next Elders meeting. Include a young person and youth leader on this task group. Refer to the Uniting Church *Young People and Your Church* policy and action manuals for further recommendations in this area.
— Ask the Elders' executive to consult with young people and youth leaders and make recommendations.
— Ask your youth ministry committee to make recommendations (you should certainly discuss it with them.)

Make sure you specify who will do what, and by what dates it is to be done, and record this in the minutes of the meeting.

Record in the meeting minutes that 'Pastoral Care of Young People' is to be on the agenda of the Council of Elders meeting in 3 or 4 months time, so that elders can share and discuss what progress has been made.

Setting up a youth ministry committee

All youth ministry needs to be co-ordinated and an effective way of doing this is for Councils of Elders to set up a youth ministry committee or task group to oversee programs and activities for young people in the church

Young People and Your Church action manual recommends:

that each local church establishes a youth ministry committee

that the youth ministry committee be appointed by the Council of Elders, responsible to that Council and through it to the congregation

that the youth ministry committee consist of approximately equal numbers of adults and young people, with representation from each group in the congregation involved with young people between 12 and 25 years, e.g. Sunday school, fun and fellowship groups, sporting teams, choirs

that the adult members of the youth ministry committee be appointed in the same way that the parish appoints members of other parish boards or committees

that the youth members of the youth ministry committee be selected by the young people they represent

that the minister, any other parish staff person with responsibility for youth ministry, and the leaders of each youth class, group, team or club should be advisory members of the youth ministry committee.

Responsibilities of the committee

Consider the following list and decide which are appropriate for your church.

● To oversee and co-ordinate the total ministry of the local church with and for young people, including classes, clubs, groups, choirs, sporting teams, service groups, evangelism, worship, service to young people in the community.
● To be aware of the needs of young people, and develop appropriate forms of ministry based on those needs.
● To support leaders in youth ministry and ensure that they are recognised and set apart by the congregation for this ministry.
● To select, recruit and nominate adult leaders for each organisation serving as part of youth ministry.
● To provide a job description for each leadership role with youth.

- To ensure that there are adequate training opportunities for leaders of youth.
- To receive and respond to regular reports from leaders of each youth organisation.
- To ensure that there are opportunities for young people to have a number of adequate adult models in the church, and to build strong personal relationships between young people and adults.
- To equip young people to fulfil their baptismal and confirmation vows, and to make sure opportunities exist for them to be full and active members of the parish.
- To make youth ministry visible in the parish, and draw to the attention of the parish the achievements, contributions and needs of young people.
- To co-ordinate the work of youth ministry with the work of other ministries in the church: evangelism, stewardship, worship, mission, service.
- To urge and oversee the regular allocation of an amount for youth ministry in the church's annual budget.
- To ensure that the church's buildings and facilities are available for youth ministry activities, and that consideration is given to appropriate settings for youth ministry.
- To expect and encourage regular attendance at church worship as a part of young people's spiritual development.
- To encourage youth participation in all aspects of the church's life, and youth involvement in the committees of the church which make decisions affecting youth ministry and young people.
- To be aware of, support and pray for the youth ministry committees and programs of Presbytery, Synod and Assembly.
- To involve parents of young people in the planning and conduct of youth ministry, and to ensure that parents are aware of specific programs and activities.
- To co-ordinate and assist with the work of sub-committees or co-ordinators of ministry with specific age groups: younger youth, older youth and young adults.

A youth ministry committee will co-ordinate your ministry to young people and make it more effective. The committee will also help set direction, evaluate and be a 'problem solving' body for youth ministry.

WORKSHEET 1: What is your church doing in youth ministry?

Tick (✓) the boxes if you are doing this already.
Put an arrow (→) in the boxes you would like to be doing more about.
Put a question mark (?) in the boxes you're not sure about.

Social justice
- ☐ Peace register
- ☐ Amnesty International
- ☐ Peace marches
- ☐ Raise money for needy
- ☐ Walk Against Want
- ☐ Prayer
- ☐ Visit prisoners

Worship
- ☐ Young people plan worship
- ☐ Devotions
- ☐ Youth services
- ☐ Regional and state worship
- ☐ Youth on worship committee
- ☐ Encourage personal devoions

Personal growth
- ☐ Help people grow in faith
- ☐ Help people grow as people
- ☐ Skills workshops
- ☐ Visitation
- ☐ Leadership, musical, craft opportunities

Evangelism
- ☐ Newsletters
- ☐ Communicating to those outside the church
- ☐ Significant events
- ☐ School evangelism

Youth participation in the church
- ☐ Young people on all decision making bodies of the church
- ☐ Young people as elders
- ☐ Young people being listened to
- ☐ Seeking opinions of young people
- ☐ Young people are valued
- ☐ Young people initiate their own programs – with support

Service
- ☐ Offer time for voluntary gardening, mow lawns, visit old people in the community
- ☐ Be available for building maintenance work for people
- ☐ Give time and labour to worthwhile organisations

Outreach
- ☐ Advertising
- ☐ Go to pubs or schools to be with kids

- ☐ After school programs
- ☐ Sports teams
- ☐ Coffee shops

Community and friendship
- ☐ Have fun – enjoy things
- ☐ Welcoming atmosphere
- ☐ Groups for all ages
- ☐ Good community feeling

Ecumenical involvement
- ☐ Worship with other denominations
- ☐ Visiting other churches
- ☐ Combined group gatherings
- ☐ Combined leaders meetings
- ☐ Interdenominational friendships

Christian education
- ☐ Cell groups
- ☐ Discussion groups
- ☐ Faith sharing groups
- ☐ Sermons
- ☐ Forums
- ☐ Christian education in schools
- ☐ Camps

How to work with young people. Copyright © 1991 The Joint Board of Christian Education.

WORKSHEET 2:   Questions to young people

What do you think young people would say if asked the following questions?

NOTE: The answers will vary for different age groups and different young people. So be general in your answers, and focus on the under 20 age group.

1. What things do you like to do?

2. What's your favourite music?

3. What are the best things about your life at the moment?

4. What do you worry about the most?

5. What questions do you hate adults to ask you?

6. What questions do you like adults to ask you?

7. How do you like to be treated by adults?

8. What are your hopes for the future?

WORKSHEET 3: Pastoral care of young people

Young people are often missed by the normal pastoral care procedures of a church. It is the responsibility of each congregation to provide pastoral care for all young people associated with the congregation. This includes young people who only attend youth groups or other youth activities, and young people not involved in the church, but whose parents are involved. It is the responsibility of the Council of Elders to ensure that pastoral care is provided for young people. But it is not necessarily their task to do it all themselves.

***Give your church a mark out of 10 for each point below according to how well you think your church is doing this at the moment (1 is the lowest score, 10 is the highest). If you don't know an answer, put a ? in the box.

Pastoral care:

1. by elders

Our Council of Elders ensures that all young people have an elder (but not the same elder for all young people).

Our Council of Elders ensures that elders actually visit the young people on their lists. This may require them making two or more visits to the one family, or having different elders for different family members (too often young people are missed by elders' visits).

2. through youth groups

Our Council of Elders ensures that all youth leaders know that providing pastoral care is part of their leadership responsibilities. Youth leaders are in the best position to know the pastoral care needs of young people and to do something about them.

Our Council of Elders appoints an elder to each youth group if none of the group's leaders are elders already. This elder should attend the group regularly.

Our Council Of Elders ensures all youth groups have adequate leadership.

Our Council of Elders ensures support and training are available for leaders.

Our Council of Elders ensures that all youth leaders know who the elders are for all their group members, so they can pass on pastoral care needs to the appropriate elder as necessary.

Our minister(s) regularly visit all youth groups in order to get to know the young people, and to support the youth leaders. Visits should be at least once a month, and the length can vary from five minutes to the entire program.

3. through representation

Our Council of Elders ensures that young people are adequately represented on the Elders Council. This may include having as elders some suitable young people, some youth leaders and some adults who are sympathetic to and in close touch with young people.

In your small groups:
a) Share your marks
b) Consider things you do which aren't listed.
c) Discuss the strengths and weaknesses of the pastoral care of young people that is provided in your church.

How to work with young people. Copyright © 1991 The Joint Board of Christian Education.

WORKSHEET 4: Lettergram

Write a lettergram to your Council of Elders saying what specific actions you believe the Council of Elders should take with regard to pastoral care of young people. Don't be restricted just to the ideas on WORKSHEET 3. What other ideas do you have?

Limit your lettergram to 16 words.

LETTERGRAM

SPECIAL INSTRUCTIONS

PLEASE USE BLOCK LETTERS

TO ....

....

.... STATE ....

....

....

....

....

....

....

FROM ....

....

Chapter 2

Participation in the church

Participation in the church

How can we co-ordinate youth ministry in our church?   25

How can young people have a say in our church?   26

How does our church work?   26

How do we get adults to support youth ministry?   29

How do we get along with our minister?   30

How do we raise money for what we want to do?   31

WORKSHEET 5: Participation checklist: young people and the church   32

WORKSHEET 6: Discussion questionnaire: young people in the life of the church   33

WORKSHEET 7: How to guarantee that young people are not a part of the church and are always a separate appendage to it (brainstorming ideas)   34

How can we co-ordinate youth ministry in our church?

Write a list of all the activities involving young people in your church:

ACTIVITY	WHO CO-ORDINATES
Youth group(s)	* Me and other leaders
* Sporting clubs	* _____
—tennis	— _____
—netball	— _____
— _____	— _____
— _____	— _____
* Sunday school	* _____
—year (age) levels	
* _____	* _____
* _____	* _____
* _____	* _____
* _____	* _____
* _____	* _____

There are often groups and activities for young people that happen with little or no communication between the groups.

Stockyard Creek – a confused story

Julie and Greg run the Stockyard Creek youth group for 15-20 year olds.

Brian and Caroline Peters run the Stockyard Creek 12-14 group.

Pat runs the tennis club and his dad Graham runs the football club.

There is a Sunday school for young people up to the end of high school – run by a variety of leaders. Greg and John have put together a basketball team of the members of the 15-20 group.

Some of the young people in the church attend more than one of the groups, but none of the events of the various groups are ever advertised when individual groups meet.

Sally, Pat's younger sister, attends all the groups, and she is probably the only person around who knows what is being offered.

On Sunday April 5th disaster struck the Stockyard Creek Church. Julie and Greg organised a camp for that weekend for the 15-20 group.

The Peters and the 12-14 group held a fund raising car wash after church. The tennis club had its club championship. There was a Sunday school family day arranged for after church.

All the leaders were annoyed because they didn't get the support they wanted for the events they planned. It occurred to the Peters that it was time to sort it all out. They rang all the leaders and invited them to dinner, to talk and look at the calendars of all the groups.

They had a great time together and decided to meet five times a year, to support each other, discuss what events are coming up for each of them, plan combined events and plug young people into the various activities from each group.

Since then the membership of each group has grown. Sally is now just one of the young people in Stockyard Creek who enjoys the wide range of activities offered.

It sounds so simple! A youth ministry committee that co-or-dinates what you do. See Chapter 1 page 17 – for a guide to setting up a youth ministry committee.

How can young people have a say in our church?

The first thing to do is to find out how the church works and where the decisions are made. Young people have a vital role to play in the church's ministry. This can be achieved through the youth ministry committee and through the councils of the church.

The Uniting Church in Australia policy *Young People and Your Church* states the following about the participation of young people in the church.

Decision-making

All gifts and abilities can enrich the church or the community. Young people need to be involved actively in the decision-making of a congregation. This means
- helping young people to understand how decisions are made in the church and how to participate in decision-making
- consulting with young people about decisions that affect them.

The Council of Elders should

- appoint elders acceptable to the young people to meet with their groups to involve them in having a say about important matters in the life and work of the church
- ensure some elders are young, or have a clear understanding of the needs and interests of young people.

Below is a picture of how the Uniting Church in Australia works at a local, regional, state and national level and points of entrance. Other denominations will have their own system.

How does our church work?

Council of Elders

The Council of Elders is basically responsible for the spiritual over-sight of the congregation. The elders are elected by the congregation. The elders are responsible for all Christian education and youth ministry which occurs within the congregation. Guidelines for Councils of Elders say, among other things, that a Council of Elders should –

Provide financial support for essential resources for teaching and leaders.

Recognise and support teachers and leaders.

Encourage teachers and leaders to participate in training events that will improve the quality of their teaching and leading.

Plan for effective ministry with youth by
- Consulting with young people to find ways in which the church can provide more effectively for spiritual needs of young people and in which young people can contribute more fully to the missions of the church.

- Appoint one or more elders to maintain regular contact between the Council of Elders and all youth groups in the congregation.
- Encourage young people's groups in the congregation to affiliate with Uniting Church young people at other levels of the church and receive regular youth mailings.

How to work with the Council of Elders:

Remind the elders of their responsibilities for youth ministry and help them find ways to carry them out.

Have suitable young people elected as elders (preferably more mature young people, as experience shows they cope better with the formal meetings).

Find sympathetic elders to stand up for young people and push youth ministry issues at the Council of Elders meetings.

Ask the elders to ratify any youth ministry appointments, and organise an annual commissioning service for all youth ministry leaders.

Report regularly about youth ministry activities and happenings and prayer requests to the elders.

Have a roster of elders who come to the youth groups and participate.

Parish Council

The parish is a group of congregations (sometimes a parish of one large congregation). The Parish Council is the overall co-ordinating body for all the congregations which make up the parish. It consists of members elected by the various congregations and the various Councils of Elders. Parish Council has particular responsibility for property and finance.

How to work with the Parish Council:

Have suitable young people elected as Parish Council members (preferably older young people).

Find sympathetic parish councillors who will stand up for young people and push youth ministry issues.

Ask them to provide a budget for youth ministry activities, leader training, etc.

Report regularly about youth ministry issues to them.

Your ministers

The minister is the theological resource person in the congregation or parish. Ministers often have ideas and resources for youth ministry just waiting to be used.

How to work with the ministers:

Ask them for ideas.

Make use of their extensive library of books and magazines.

When in doubt about how the system works, ask the minister to explain it to you.

Pick the minister's brain for worship ideas.

Invite the minister along to some youth ministry activities so the kids can get to know him/her.

The minister can be a very important political ally, so make sure he/she is kept informed about and on side with all youth ministry happenings.

Meet regularly and give all the ministers a youth ministry program.

Parish Council and Council of Elders sub-committees

Both councils have various sub-committees such as property and finance, social justice, Christian education, evangelism, Sunday school.

How to work with the sub-committees:

Try to get appropriate young people on the various committees. Ensure that committees that relate directly to youth ministry have young people involved.

Many of the previous suggestions apply here also.

Youth ministry committee

Each congregation should have a youth ministry committee which has oversight for all youth ministry in the congregation.

How to work with the youth ministry committee:

As well as co-ordinating various youth ministry activities, the youth ministry committee should act as a watch dog to ensure that the other councils of the church take their responsibilities for youth ministry seriously e.g. write letters to them; have young people as members, etc.

Presbytery

The Presbytery is the regional co-ordinating council. It is made up of ministers and parish delegates from each parish in the region. It has oversight of all parishes and ministers and has various committees such as worship, Christian education, social justice, theological students, property.

All presbyteries should have Presbytery Youth Advisory Councils or their equivalent, which co-ordinate youth ministry in the Presbytery.

How to work with Presbytery:

Make sure there are some young people who are members of Presbytery.

Ensure that you and your youth groups are on the presbytery youth mailing list.

Make sure that you and your youth groups attend all the relevant presbytery youth events.

Get to know the other youth leaders in your immediate area, so that you can call on them for ideas, support, etc. Do some combined activities with their groups.

Find sympathetic presbytery members to stand up for young people and push youth ministry issues.

Ask presbyteries to meet at a time young people can attend (if they don't already).

Synod

The Synod is the state level co-ordinating councils of the Uniting Church. The Synod meets annually and is made up of ministers and lay people. It has oversight of the Uniting Churches ministry in the state, and has various committees, divisions and boards.

How to work with Synod:

Ensure that some youth people from your presbytery are elected to attend the annual synod meeting.

Become familiar with the resources of the youth unit. Attend leadership training events; encourage your young people to attend the camps; ring up when you need ideas; etc.

Make sure that you are on the youth unit's mailing list to receive information during the year.

Assembly

The Assembly is the national co-ordinating body for the Uniting Church. The Assembly meets every three years, and also has various councils and committees such as the Council for Christian Education, Ministerial Education, Mission, The Joint Board of Christian Education which is the national co-ordinator for youth ministry.

How to work with Assembly:

Subscribe to *A.D.* magazine and *A.D. Leader's Guide* from the Joint Board of Christian Education.

Read the Joint Board books and resource lists that they put out from time to time in Youth Unit mailings, to keep up to date with the latest ideas, books and resources.

Other tips for working within the system

Ensure that young people who are selected for various councils or committees of the church are people who have a contribution to make to that committee and are not just 'token' young people.

Experience has shown that more mature young people (about 20-25 years) are best able to cope with the more formal meeting structure of the church.

When putting young people on councils or committees, some time needs to be spent explaining to them how committees actually work, for example, what the procedures are. It is a good idea to have a sympathetic, more experienced campaigner sit next to the young people for the first few meetings to help them understand what is going on.

Organise some all-age activities for the congregation from time to time such as parent dinners, family picnics and barbecues, Sunday school picnics, old time dances, all age discussion groups, parish concerts. If the adults and young people know each other from social settings, they are less likely to be suspicious of each other, and the adults are more likely to be supportive of young people in youth ministry.

Make sure there are regular articles about the youth ministry activities of the congregation in the congregational magazine.

Have a youth ministry notice board at the door way into the church. Keep it up to date with what is happening.

Make a list of people in the church who are willing to be occasional resource people or helpers for youth ministry activities. This will provide support for youth leaders, as well as increase the number of people in the congregation who are informed about and supportive of youth ministry.

Have question and answer panels with key church leaders.

Set up a talent bank of parent and church member skills etc.

Have an annual meeting of the parents of young people to explain what you do, help your needs, and answer questions.

For further information and ways to encourage young people to 'be heard', a video and work booklet has been produced called *'Saying Something – Being Heard*. This video is for sale from the Joint Board of Christian Education, 10 Queen Street, Melbourne 3000. Ph: (03) 629 5076, and from most Uniting Church Synod offices.

How do we get adults in the church to support youth ministry?

Often all you need to do is ask.

Often you need to help the older members of the church see that they have gifts and skills to offer. Often you need to help them see that what they are doing may not be helpful to young people.

The church needs to be aware that young people need as much support and nurture as older people. It is useful to set up dialogue between young people,

youth leaders and the adults in the church.

Strategies to use in dialogue

1. Begin by celebrating the good things in the local church, and affirming some aspects of life in the congregation.

2. Have people write or draw their own visions for the church using topics such as 'The church I want', 'The church we want', 'The church God wants'. Share in small groups.

3. How we see it. Divide into two groups; young people in one group, adults in a second. (If these groups are too big, sub-divide.) Have each group discuss these topics:
   a) How we see ourselves participating in the fellowship, worship and mission of our church.
   b) How we see the other group participating in the fellowship, worship and mission of the church.

c) How we think the other groups see us participating in the fellowship, worship and mission of our church.

4. Agendas
   a) Divide into two groups: young people in one group, all other ages in a second. (If these groups are too big, sub-divide.)
   Task: each group is to work together to develop an agenda of four topics to be discussed with one person from the other group.
   b) Bring groups back together, pair them off (if numbers are uneven, put two of one group with one from the other group).
   Task: each pair is to discuss agendas together, going all the way through one agenda before beginning the second.

5. Check list. Divide into groups (same age or cross-age groups) and prepare a short check list which indicates real involvement in the fellowship, worship and mission of the church. Swap check lists and complete another group's list

in terms of your own local church.

6. Slides. As a prelude to discussion, prepare box meals of some kind for about six people each (e.g. cut sandwiches). Pair young people and ask them to choose two or three adults (whatever the number allows) with whom to share their meal. During or after the meal, show some slides which picture the young people's activities in the church and the community. Follow with slides showing the adults' activities in the church and the community. Have the group who shared a meal together discuss what each one does within the church, what committees they serve on, what programs they are involved in, etc. To conclude, read Ephesians 2:11-22.

7. Use the check list and questions provided (WORK-SHEETS 5 and 6) to promote discussion in a mixed age group.

8. Have everyone 'brainstorm' a list of ideas – 'How to guarantee that young people are not a part of the church and are always a separate appendage to it' (see WORKSHEET 7 for some previously brainstormed ideas).

How do we get along with our ministers?

Stockyard Creek – yet another confused story

Julie, Greg, the Peters, Pat and his dad and the Sunday school teachers had been meeting as the Parish Youth Ministry Committee for about 6 months. They had actually taken a recommendation to the councils of the church for their committee to become official.

On Tuesday night, October 6th, it looked like a crisis was looming. The Youth Ministry Committee was meeting and the minister, the Rev. J. Mitchell, came to the meeting. Twelve months ago, the Rev. J. Mitchell's youngest child, Grant, had left Stockyard Creek to go to university. Grant had been heavily involved in the 15-20 youth group and the tennis club.

The Rev. J. Mitchell came to say that since Grant had left, there were fewer young people dropping in and as Grant had been such a good source for what was happening in the youth group, he was no longer there to inform his parents of activities.

The Rev. J. Mitchell was missing the contact with young people and wanted to know, from the Youth Ministry Committee, what help was required.

This is what they came up with – add your own.
— Give the Rev. J. Mitchell a syllabus of every group.
— Work out events and times that the Rev. J. Mitchell could attend.
— Have a morning tea with the young people once every two months after the worship service for the minister to get feed back and meet any new faces.
— Ask the Rev. J. Mitchell to 'at least' drop into the youth events once a month to say 'hi'.

— The leaders will inform the minister of any significant things that happen.
— Ask the Rev. J. Mitchell to speak at one of the events.

— ....

— ....

— ....

It was a good thing that the minister came to the Youth Ministry Committee. In some churches, it will be the other way around, but the strategy would remain the same – meet with the minister to set up a strategy for information sharing, support and helping the young people know and understand the minister (and vice-versa).

How do we raise money for what we want to do?

By rights the church should add the needs of young people and their activities into its yearly budget. The group should be allocated a sum for its use during the year. The youth group should also raise money for the church and its projects. Below are some ways of 'getting money' and 'getting rid' of money.

GETTING MONEY

* A budget allocation from the church.
* Weekly subs from members.
* Fund raising activities
  — concerts
  — food drives
  — craft making/selling
  — car washes
  — gardening/cleaning
* Government funding. Some State governments offer local grants for youth activities, all it needs is a submission to the correct department. Contact your State Department of Youth Affairs and enquire into funding.

GETTING RID OF MONEY

* Encourage individual young people in the group to be better stewards with their money and help them set a sum they think would be appropriate for themselves.
* Check what projects your church or the wider church needs money for and raise funds.
* Buy equipment that can be used by the whole church.
* Check what areas of need there are in your local community and enthuse the group into supporting those areas.

WORKSHEET 5: Participation checklist – young people and the church

Mark each statement with your response:

✓ We are doing this well.
x We are doing this poorly or not at all.
? Not sure about this.

☐ Young people are involved in every part of the life of the church.

☐ Young people are members of our church's committees.

☐ Young people serve on our Council of Elders

☐ Young people serve on our Parish Council.

☐ Meetings in our church are scheduled at a time when young people are able to attend.

☐ Adults other than youth leaders want young people to take leadership roles in the life of the church.

☐ We have an active youth ministry committee or other committee with responsibility for youth ministry in our church.

☐ Our youth committee or other committee with responsibility for youth ministry includes both young people and adults.

☐ Young people enjoy their participation in the life of our church.

☐ One or more groups for young people meet weekly.

☐ We plan for and involve younger youth (12-14 year olds) in our church's fellowship, worship and mission.

☐ We plan for and involve older youth (15-17 year olds) in our church's fellowship, worship and mission.

☐ We plan for and involve young adults (18-25 year olds) in our church's fellowship, worship and mission.

☐ Young people and adults study social issues and work together on service projects in our church.

☐ Our church offers experiences such as camps to encourage a sense of fellowship and belonging for people of all ages.

☐ Young people can and do serve as leaders in our church

☐ We encourage young people to express their ideas and concerns.

☐ Adults in our church share their faith with young people.

☐ Our church helps young people to understand what it means to be a Christian, through confirmation classes and Bible study.

☐ Our church encourages young people to commit their lives to Jesus Christ through church membership, attendance and worship, and stewardship.

☐ Our church expects young people to participate in all parts of our church's fellowship, worship and mission.

☐ Our church plans ways to contact young people who have never participated in our church's fellowship, worship and mission.

☐ Our church plans ways to contact young people who no longer participate in our church's fellowship, worship and mission.

WORKSHEET 6: Discussion questionnaire: young people in the life of the church

1. What do you understand to be the meaning of the phrase 'young people participating in the worship, fellowship and mission of the church'? (Tick more than one, if you wish, and add any other meanings not listed).

☐ Young people being represented on church councils and committees.

☐ Young people being respected as individuals on church councils and committees.

☐ The voice of young people being heard by church councils and committees.

☐ Young people running their own show.

☐ Young people being involved in events and programs which interest them.

☐ (other)..

....

☐ (other)..

....

☐ (other)..

....

2. Do you think young people always have the skills and abilities to participate in the worship, fellowship and mission of the church?

....

....

....

....

....

....

3. Do you believe young people want to participate in the worship, fellowship and mission of the church?

☐ Yes

☐ No

☐ Only occasionally

☐ Only some young people

4. What do you think young people want from the worship, fellowship and mission of the church?

....

....

....

....

....

....

....

....

....

....

....

....

....

How to work with young people. Copyright © 1991 The Joint Board of Christian Education.

33

WORKSHEET 7: How to guarantee that young people are not a part of the church and are always a separate appendage to it (brainstorming ideas)

- Have a strict code about what young people wear to church.
- Appoint a bored, unsatisfied youth worker to 'do the job'.
- Give them token positions in the church (for instance, Youth Service means they take up the offering).
- By-pass teenagers in passing the peace.
- Always talk about them as 'the church of tomorrow'.
- Spend thousands of dollars on other things, like buildings, then tell young people there's no money for youth affairs.
- Put youth affairs last on the Parish agenda, then when it arises, say it's too late and time is gone.
- Lock up the Ladies Guild's saucers, cups and coffee.
- Be as critical of young people as possible.
- Have them meet in the Kindergarten room, with little chairs.
- Don't let young people EVER think they have the right to speak to a person with a position of authority in the life of the church.
- Always have an important church anniversary or service on the same weekend as a key youth event.
- Conduct all Parish meetings in parliamentary style.
- Don't encourage questions from young people.
- Hold a congregational meeting and send young people out to kick a football.
- Have youth camps but never family camps.
- Complain about the state of church halls after they've been there.
- Never provide anything past Sunday school, but if you do, call it Sunday school.
- Never refer to youth ministry in news sheets, prayer rosters, announcements, annual reports, church papers.
- Never pray for OR with young people.
- When a young Christian comes to your church, put them straight on a committee.
- Never expect young people to be involved in any area except the youth group.
- Ask young people what they think, listen to what they say, then ignore it.
- Make Sunday school a real failure so they drop out before they become youth.
- Tell them you don't like their friends.
- Never give them a place of their own to meet in.
- Insist all youth group activities are funded by young people themselves.
- Boycott youth worship services.

Chapter 3

Recruiting leaders

Recruiting leaders

How do we encourage new leaders to volunteer?   37

Recruitment: a model   37

Growing your own leaders   38

How do we keep good leaders?   38

WORKSHEET 8: Considering a possible leader   40

WORKSHEET 9: An ideal leader   41

How do we encourage new leaders to volunteer?

There once lived a man who needed some help to do what he thought would change the world. You would think that he would have gone to the most powerful people in his area to help him. You would think he would have spent a lot of time convincing anybody to help him. Instead this is what he did:

*** Read Matthew 4:18-22 ***

This is an example of Jesus recruiting people.

What can we learn about recruitment from Jesus' example?

(You might list the things you learn.)

....

....

....

....

....

....

....

Why do people lead? What motivates them?

1. Genuine desire to help people and do Christian service.

2. It's an opportunity to offer and use their skills.

3. To satisfy personal needs.

People are more likely to be willing to take on a voluntary task, and even be enthusiastic about doing so if:
— it is a significant task
— it will enable them to experience personal and/or Christian growth
— there is a support system in place
— the task promises to be enjoyable and satisfying

— their responsibilities will increase as their skills and
— experience increase
— the task has a fixed time limit
— they will not be working alone.
—
—
—

Which (if any) of the above motivated you to be a leader?

Will what encouraged you to lead, encourage others?

Looking for the leader who is 'just right'

There is never a perfect person for the job of youth leadership, but there are ways of finding people who have some of the right qualities. When searching for a new leader, outside of the group, use WORKSHEETS 8 and 9 to help.

Recruitment: a model

Decide who should do the recruiting, who should be consulted, represented, make decisions, etc.

Define and list the responsibilities of the position – what needs to be done.

List the skills required to carry out the task.

Define and list the opportunities and satisfactions that the position would offer those undertaking it.

Consider and list the support and possible training opportunities for people undertaking the position.

Write a job description listing:
— position title
— skills required
— term of appointment
— specific duties
— support provided
— training
— opportunities for review
— etc.

Consider and list strategies for finding the person or people to undertake the position.

Identify suitable people for the position.

Approach and interview possible people.

Select a person or persons.

Commission the person or people into the service they have undertaken.

* See 'Making Groups Work' Chapter 5 for a simulation game that may be helpful in identifying potential leaders.

A Christian leader must express a dimension to leadership not always evident in secular leadership. This is a spiritual dimension and is a deeply personal thing – a presence.

Paul told Timothy to keep spiritually fit and that his whole life must bear out what he taught others.

A Christian leader needs also to be aware of the importance of regularly using the 'means of grace' – prayer, daily Scripture readings, Christian fellowship, worship and participation in the sacraments.

Growing your own leaders

The aim of older groups should be to grow their own leaders from the young people who attend the group. This is a continuous process and involves developing the leadership potential of youth group members.

Here are some principles for developing leadership in your own group members:

Never plan anything by yourself – always invite young people from the group to help plan, run and evaluate a program.

Rotate – use different young people all the time, never over-use one or two. Always give as many people as possible a job.

Check that those in the group who have special skills are being encouraged to use their talents (e.g. music, photography, drama, speaking).

Encourage potential leaders to participate in events outside your group – this will give new ideas, widen their vision, offer alternative models for youth leadership.

How do we train leaders?

Apprenticeship training as mentioned above is one of the best training models – see a leader, do with the leader, be a leader.

There are other, more formal ways to train leaders. Many courses and experiences are available, run by your own church or other churches and agencies.

The advantages of an outside training course or event are countless. Attendance at a leadership training event will offer:

● meeting points between your leaders and other leaders (for support)
● sharing of ideas and resources
● quality discussion on aspects of youth leadership that everyone finds difficult
● basic theory on the 'whys' of youth leadership
● a feeling that 'we are not doing this alone'.

Training courses are run by most denominations (check your regional and state bodies) plus agencies like Scripture Union.

Training courses cost money and it in is your church's interest to pay some if not all of the registration cost for a leader to attend a training event. Check with your church's governing body to see if each year they will set aside funds for youth leader training.

How do we keep good leaders?

Once there was a man who gathered good people around him to help him do what he thought would change the world. The people he gathered were a diverse group, all with different skills. He encouraged them to develop their skills and use them. Just before he left them to continue the work without him, this is what he said:

*** Read Matthew 28:16-20 ***

Jesus supported
        encouraged
        cared
        nurtured
        helped
        re-assured
        complimented
        critically evaluated
        never said 'it's up to you,
          you're own your own.'

We can learn much from Jesus about the way he led and the way he recruited and trained.

If we support, care for and encourage our leaders, we will have a vital team that will do the same for us and others.

What are the things that others do for you that keep you going and motivated for leadership?

*

*

*

*

*

*

*

These are the first keys to keeping good leaders.

NOW – ask your new leaders what helps them and DO IT!

WORKSHEET 8: Considering a possible leader

Fill in this sheet with the leadership team. First complete the sentence beginning 'A leader ought...' in each key area. Then decide whether the person you are considering has the gifts you feel are necessary to be a leader.

NAME:...

KEY AREAS	NOT YET	UNSURE	PROBABLY	YES
FAITH A leader ought				
RELATIONSHIPS A leader ought				
MATURITY A leader ought				
GIFTS A leader ought				
WILLINGNESS TO GROW A leader ought to				
AVAILABILITY A leader ought				
OTHER A leader ought				

WORKSHEET 9: An ideal leader

Put a tick against the 5 statements that are most important.

AN IDEAL LEADER IS ONE WHO

☐ Sees each person as having worth and dignity in his/her own right.

☐ Respects people enough not to intrude upon their privacy.

☐ Does not force people to speak.

☐ Does not tell others to participate, but creates a situation in which they can participate.

☐ Helps people to really communicate with one another.

☐ Believes each member of the group has something to say worth hearing.

☐ Is a good listener and one who encourages people not just to hear, but to listen carefully to what others are trying to say.

☐ Is patient and gently draws people out and assists them in becoming articulate.

☐ Does not manipulate the group to agree with or follow his/her ideas.

☐ Is not self-seeking.

☐ Is flexible, but not casual; sensitive to the mood and expressed needs of the group.

☐ Is the servant of the group and not the boss.

☐ Has warmth, understanding and an easy manner.

☐ Makes all his/her life available to the group.

☐ Does not expect to be a perfect leader. Remembers a few fundamental guides and tries to use them to start with.

42

Chapter 4

Leadership development

Leadership development

How do I grow spiritually?   45

What sort of qualities should I work on – and
leave behind?   47

What are some of the common errors in youth
leadership?   47

What are the characteristics of effective
leadership?   48

How can adults communicate with young people?   50

How do we build a strong leadership team?   52

Are team dynamics important?   53

How do I get everything done on time?   54

WORKSHEET 10: Things to do today   55

WORKSHEET 11: Weekly planner sheet   56

How do I grow spiritually?

Six areas of input could be described as the priority needs of youth leaders for spiritual growth. The correct amount of each will not guarantee perfect operation – but will certainly enhance the end product!

1. Prayer

Too often prayer is seen as an output – something we do for God or to God. In fact, God is always there, waiting to have fellowship with us, and all we need do is turn aside to spend time with God. 'Come near to God and he will come near to you' (James 4:8).

God obviously puts a great deal of confidence in us in giving us a leading role. Let's make it obvious who is really in charge by talking all the important decisions through with God.

Others need to pray for us too. If people in the church have not thought of praying for you and your work as youth leader, why not ask them? Such a prayer-covenant can have many other spin-offs.

2. Bible study

Like the children of Israel in the desert, the busy youth leader can fall into the trap of believing that a full stomach is sufficient sustenance for the task ahead. As Moses pointed out, people must not depend on bread alone to sustain them, but on everything the Lord says. (Deuteronomy 8:3)

The reading of God's word will provide us with many benefits and perhaps the greatest of these will be the wisdom to lead our youth group. Note, however, the distinction between wisdom and knowledge. Some youth leaders are quite brilliant in technique and skill, but a wise youth leader knows what is important in the life of the group and will act appropriately in all circumstances.

'I understand more than all my teachers because I meditate on your instructions. I have greater wisdom than old men because I obey your commands' (Psalm 119:99-100). A Big Mac is no substitute for reading the Word.

3. Guidance

The question of guidance is resolved in greater part by the two previous issues. 'Your word is a lamp to guide me and a light for my path' (Psalm 119:105).

A third source of guidance is the collective prayerful consideration of the body of believers with whom you have fellowship. The old saying 'two heads are better than one' can be modified to read 'a collection of people with one head – Jesus Christ – is the best of all'. Find a group to support you in your work; other Christians to counsel you, talk things over with, feed in ideas and, most of all, support you with their prayers.

4. Lifestyle

The whole question of leadership, which includes the issue of knowing God's will for our actions, is a matter of faith. Our lives should be models, not of excellence or talent, but of faith. Only by faith can we have any confidence that anything we do is acceptable before God. If we've already trusted God for our eternal life it should only be a small thing to trust God in day to day living.

God's objective is to make us 'like Jesus' (Romans 8:29). Obviously, being holy enough for God is something we alone cannot do. We could not save ourselves; neither can we make ourselves like Christ. It is God who will renew our minds (Romans 12:2) and make us the kind of youth leaders who will communicate Christ to the young people we lead.

5. Creativity

As youth leaders we must constantly be fine-tuning the gifts which we have been given. First, we need to make use of the training which is available to us. Churches, government departments and colleges all offer programs which will develop our leadership abilities. We need to strive to maximise the effectiveness of the work we do by being well equipped and resourced.

Second, we need to put time into our planning and preparation. To roll up to our youth group unprepared, or with a program that has been just thrown together, shows a distinct lack of love for those we lead. It is presumptuous to expect the Holy Spirit to cover up for our lack of preparation.

6. Relationships

As Christians we fall into two families outside our own biological or marital group of fathers, mothers, brothers, sisters, husbands, wives and children. We are members of the family of God. We all have the same heavenly Father, we are all saved by the same Christ, and therefore we are all brothers and sisters in a very real sense. The quality of this relationship will be of great importance to our work as youth leaders. 'Don't do anything from selfish ambition or from a cheap desire to boast, but be humble towards one another, always considering others better than yourselves' (Philippians 2:3). Jesus Christ gave us a great lesson in leadership when he washed the disciples' feet. For him, to lead was to empty himself for others. This is our example to follow.

We are also members of the family of humanity. We cannot ignore Jesus' concern for the poor in situation and spirit. From our example, those we lead will learn what their relationships with others are to be like. Have we non-Christian friends to whom we relate as friends and as Christians, or do we only know those in the church? Do we, as the story says, 'love our neighbour' as we love ourselves? (Luke 10:27).

Jesus' final instructions were to go throughout the whole world and preach the gospel to all people (Mark 16:15). We are called to be evangelists, not just youth leaders.

Our priority as youth leaders is to take in, in terms of our own spiritual, professional and personal lives, so that we might give out. It seems a daunting task. How can who we are and what we do be acceptable to God? But, as Paul shared confidently with the Thessalonians, God who calls us will do it because God is faithful (1 Thessalonians 5:24).

12 golden rules for youth leaders

1. Know yourself
This means knowing your own strengths, weaknesses, crisis-points, etc. And it means knowing your motives for being involved in youth work.

2. Be prepared to live at risk
When you are dealing with young people, you need to meet them on their terms rather than yours. You have to allow yourself to be vulnerable without feeling threatened or insecure.

3. Have the capacity to love people
You need to place the needs of others before your own. But you also need to love others as you do yourself – so it takes both elements. This is as true for the 'unlovely' kids as for those who are easy to love.

4. Be prepared to assess your motives
Youth work may partially meet our needs for esteem and acceptance, or even our sexual needs. We have to be prepared to be honest about our motives so that they don't interfere with our work. And likewise, when we recognise a call to youth work, we need to hang on to it despite any pressures we may face.

5. Seek the gift of wisdom
James 3:13-18 gives us an outline of what wisdom is. It is interesting to see that it involves being peacemakers.

6. Be enthusiastic
'If the trumpet makes an uncertain sound, how shall we know when to go to battle?' And with enthusiasm comes optimism.

7. Be socially aware and socially committed
Mission is a lifestyle, not a part-time job.

8. Have a point of solitude or reflection
We all need space to withdraw, reflect and recuperate.

9. Have the concept of being a servant
Youth work is itself a vocation and not a stepping stone to some 'higher' ministry. The role of the servant is to assist others in their personal growth.

10. Be makers of disciples
This can be particularly difficult when working with street kids because of the cultural gap between them and the church.

11. Be prepared to be let down again and again
Don't let disappointments break you or your service to others. And don't disappoint others unless you have no other choice.

12. Be disciplined
— know the needs of your people
— be an example
— allow expression
— find a spiritual director or support group
— be a servant.

What sort of qualities should I work on – and leave behind?

A leader should not be

- ... *a person who takes on the job for the wrong reasons*; who is on an ego trip, looking for admiration and trying to build a following; the 'personality' man or woman who counts on this to get through the session, rather than on thorough preparation.
- ... *insensitive*; does not take the trouble to really work at developing meaningful relationships with the group. This requires real effort on the part of leaders.
- ... *the boss* – always directing the show. This person dominates the discussion, suppressing all that doesn't fit into his or her own ideas, experiences and understanding.
- ... *disgruntled*. If people have to be talked into doing the job they may find it is the right role for them after all or they may bitterly regret allowing themselves to be persuaded into taking it on. If they do not enjoy leadership they may be overly critical, perhaps cynical. They wont be happy or find it fulfilling. This attitude is quickly reflected in the members of the group.
- ... *always talking*. It is often the most articulate person who is chosen as a group leader. Sometimes this choice is the wrong one. The person who quickly grasps the subject and is able to communicate ideas is useful, but is sometimes impatient of the people who are thinking more slowly. It is easier to do all the talking than any real listening.
- ... *too casual*. The group is told to get on with the discussion; a word of encouragement is given now and then but little or no direction.
- ... *shockable and unloving*. So often in groups there is pressure to conform, to say the right thing. People don't have the nerve to admit they don't agree with something, or have a different idea of things, in case they are howled down – or worse – considered stupid or sinful.

What are some of the common errors in youth leadership?

1. Barren program

To meet the varying needs of participants, the program should be as rich and varied as possible. Too often youth group programs get in a rut. There is a need to continually introduce new ideas, activities and original ways of presenting old activities. Too often the program is limited by the leader's skills – don't be afraid to use outside people with new skills. If the program isn't stimulating, young people will seek their entertainment elsewhere.

2. Poor group practices

a) Exclusive use of one form of group activity, large or small. A good variety of approaches is desirable.

b) Failure to take personalities and abilities into account when structuring groups. e.g. Putting expert basketballers with novices who already have feelings of inferiority and inadequacy.

c) If you make changes, consider how the needs of the group will lead participants to act in the new combinations.

3. Authoritarian control

Telling everyone what, when and how to do things, and not being open to criticism or other's views of how things could be done.

Authoritarian leadership usually means:

a) People react by being either submissive or aggressive and both of these are not healthy.

b) There is high productivity – the group may achieve a lot – but there is a lot of resentment and bad feeling in the group.

c) When the leader is absent, group productivity and control drops.

4. 'Laissez-faire' organisation

(Opposite to authoritarian control)

a) Lets a group drift without any direction.

b) Participants openly show boredom.

c) There are no clear limits and direction to behaviour, making frustration, fighting and general misbehaviour more likely.

5. Exploiting youth

a) Using the group as the means for satisfying one's own needs.

b) Instituting programs, approaches that are designed to win approval from adults, outsiders rather than satisfy the group.

6. Tight or exclusive in-groups

The leader may work hard to develop a strong core group pride, but in so doing may encounter two kinds of trouble.

a) There may be resentment, bickering and tension between the group and other young people.

b) Self-pride in the core group may lead to formal membership requirements or informal restrictions to limit the activities of the privileged few.

7. False atmosphere

Groups with an enthusiastic leader may appear to be enjoying themselves, but when alone express their boredom and frustration. Participants use the group for purposes different from those they say or the leaders expect.

8. Ignoring local subcultures

There is a need to be sensitive to local attitudes, customs and ways of doing things. We must realize that our own personal value system is not universal.

What are the characteristics of effective leadership?

1. **The capacity for caring about young people** is essential. A sense of duty or loyalty to the minister is not sufficient reason for agreeing to work with young people. We must care about them as persons.

   This kind of caring grows from our understanding of God's love for all people and the joyous meaning that comes from choosing to respond to that love. This is neither sentiment nor self-righteousness but a giving of oneself in specific relationships. It means that we are willing to be present to these young people; that we are supportive of them in their struggles toward maturity; that we see them as individuals.

   Caring is quite basic. If we cannot care about them, then we ought to have enough Christian integrity to serve the church in some other capacity. And the local church should have enough Christian integrity to make sure that the leaders of its youth groups really do care about young people, as a group and as individuals.

2. **Openness, flexibility, and honesty** are important in youth ministry. We need to be open to each other, to new possibilities for carrying out youth ministry, to fresh ideas and the exploration of relevant issues, to having our own prejudices and weaknesses uncovered, to the future, and above all to the leading of God's Spirit.

   We need to be flexible about ways of doing things, flexible towards change when it seems necessary and appropriate, flexible in the midst of demands made on young people by schools, family, and community involvements.

   Effective youth leaders need to be honest with themselves, asking such questions as: Why did I agree to work with this group? What are my personal assets for the job? What are my weak spots? How can I work on the weak ones and constructively use the strong ones? Can I drop some of my masks and let the group members see me as I really am?

We need to be honest as we work with younger youth. We do not have all the answers – nor all the questions! The young people suspect as much and deep down we know that. Therefore, let's be free enough to admit it. We are not called by God to 'play games' with them; we are called to be lovingly honest.

3. **The ability to listen** has no substitute. Take young people seriously. Hear what they are saying. Read between the lines of talk – what they do not say is often as significant as their words. It is important not to prejudge them, but to listen with open minds and receptive hearts. Yes, they may offer excessive opinions that are more feelings than facts, they may generalise around the real issues, they may over-react (we all do that at times!), but listening sensitively can help adults to know how to help young people uncover facts to go with feelings, sharpen up the issues, and find appropriate reactions.

4. A youth group leader needs to **act in an adult manner**. Many churches have young people as leaders because they feel this appropriate. But 12-14/15 year olds want and need the security of a mature leader. However they do not want adults who move into their culture to the extent of trying to dress, talk and act as they do. Since adults are not 12-14/15 year olds, it is a mistaken notion to adopt their current language, styles of dress, tastes in music or latest fads of any kind in order to be able to communicate with them. It is good to understand these parts of their sub-culture, but we need only to be who we are, at the same time as we allow young people to be who they are.

5. **Skill in knowing how to lead without dominating**, to guide by helping others to take hold, is important. An adult, a leader, does have a role within youth ministry. This is especially true in ministry with younger youth. There are two extremes to be avoided. One is the role of just being there – sitting or observing without really participating. The other extreme is the tendency to take over, to run things, to dominate, to do everything, to impose a pattern. Often this pattern is designed to meet our own needs, or repeat our own experiences in a youth group some years ago.

Instead, let us think of ourselves as enablers. The dictionary reminds us that to enable means 'to make able, to make possible, practical, or easy'. As leaders, we are to help others take hold, to be instruments through which the group can build its own life, to be agents or catalysts through whom good things can happen. Likely as not, in

the very process we, too, are enabled!

6. **Awareness of our continuing need to struggle and grow** in the faith keeps us mindful of our ongoing life as Christians. The gospel is the source of youth ministry. Therefore it has to have international relevance in our lives. Who we are as struggling, growing Christians cannot be separated from who we are as leaders of youth groups.

What younger youth would like in youth group leaders

From research projects in Australia and overseas and the experience of youth leaders it is possible to gain an idea of what younger youth would like from the leaders and programs of their church youth groups. Here are some of the things young people have said:

* I'd like to tell them, please do not be scared of us.

* We need freedom to discuss what's important to us right now.
* Please don't cut off our conversation, or squelch us, all for the sake of the program, or because it's not what you want to do.
* Say what you mean and mean what you say.
* If you are comfortable with us, we can feel it. If you are not comfortable, we can feel that too, and then we're uncomfortable.

* Don't automatically assume we will be difficult or hostile or non co-operative. And don't believe us every time we show initial lack of enthusiasm. Take time to 'sell' things to us and if you have complaints, back them up with facts.
* Act like an adult.

Young people thrive best where the leader shows interest and confidence in them by helping them to decide on what to do.

The good leader builds a successful and happy group atmosphere by:
1) letting others have a say and a meaningful role
2) sharing know-how without giving orders
3) being an example, taking part in and enjoying activities
4) delegating responsibilities, not allowing themselves to do everything and make the group dependent on the leader. The group can carry on effectively when the leader is absent.

How can adults communicate with young people?

Earning the right to speak

The problem:
Many people find it difficult to communicate in a deep and meaningful way with young people and are reluctant to accept leadership tasks.

Some approaches:
1. Some try to get 'where young people are at' in their experience of life and in their language. Sometimes they find it hard to move past this into the area of sharing the faith, because they find it hard to find the appropriate language and expression; for example, trying to explain what sin is without using the word 'sin'. This group seems to believe that knowing youth culture and speaking to it in its own language is a sufficient background for trying to share the gospel.

2. At the other extreme is the straight 'evangelical jargon' approach which in many cases is like a foreign language to non-church young people and fails to communicate the essence of the gospel. Supporters of this approach often don't see the need to understand or get to know people before they share the gospel and see no need for any training in communication skills.

Somewhere between these is the area of meaningful communication. Clearly when we speak to young people it is essential to:
i. understand ourselves – our values, beliefs, habits
ii. understand them and be able to communicate this understanding to them
iii. be able to be understood when we speak to them.

We may well ask the question: Where do we look for the answers to some of our communication problems?

Much research has been carried out to try and discover what it is that contributes to good communication, good relationships and the possibility of personal betterment and development.

There is extensive evidence to suggest that a central core of personality characteristics possessed by some people help them establish communication and good relationships, while those with low levels of these characteristics don't improve relationships or even make them worse. It seems that, rather than being techniques or methods, these characteristics represent integrated parts of the human personality. This helps to explain why many trained counsellors are less effective than some skilled lay people.

The core characteristics found are:

Empathy 'getting inside the person's shoes'; accurately understanding the other person's frame of reference and being able to communicate that understanding to them.

Respect the feeling and communication of unconditional regard for the other person; involves warmth, spontaneity and an effort to understand.

Genuineness 'being real;' being aware of who you are in the relationship; being consistent and honest.

Concreteness operating in the here and now; not only delving into the past or future; sharing how you think and feel NOW.

Self-disclosure (related to genuineness) freely volunteering your personal ideas, attitudes and experiences to others.

Confrontation giving feedback to the person; confronting the other person with inconsistencies or discrepancies in their behaviour.

(The last two are most effective in the more developed stages of relationships)

On the basis of this model it would seem that people who are able to initiate and maintain healthy relationships with open and fruitful communication are people who provide high levels of empathy, respect, genuineness, etc.

A Christian view

If we, as Christians, are to be intellectually honest we must recognise these findings as worthy of note and attempt to develop the kinds of characters and skills that will enable others to feel understood, respected and worthwhile persons in their relationship with us.

However, even if these are the basic elements that provide the climate for developing meaningful relationships, they tell us little of the underlying motivations. We enter into relationships partly to satisfy our own needs (we were meant to be in relationships with others). Ultimately we may want to share the faith that means so much to us. However, for the Christian the main reason that people are so important to us is that we are enabled to recognise their individual worthwhileness and integrity as God's unique creations. We are able to respond to them in love because of God's love as we know it through our relationship with Jesus. That Jesus was prepared to die so that we could be God's friends (2 Corinthians 5:20) gives us some idea of the possible costs in relationships.

It is in the context of our relationship with God that we ultimately find the key to our relationships with others (see 1 John 4:19-21).

It is worthwhile looking to the life of Jesus for a basis for meaningful relationships and communication with people.

In Jesus' relationships with others as we see them in the New Testament he:
— always made an effort to really understand others
— was always truly himself and consistent in thought, word and deed
— treated others with dignity as worthwhile persons no matter what they had done
— operated in the here and now. He didn't dwell on the past and its problems and concerns but related meaningfully to the person's present situation and circumstances.
— shared himself; who he was, where he came from, what he thought.
— was not afraid to confront others with the inconsistency in their lives or to speak the truth.

Hence, it is possible to recognise the high levels of the core personality characteristics in Jesus' life (empathy, genuineness, respect, concreteness, self-disclosure, confrontation). However, this would not seem a sufficient explanation for the changes that Jesus was able to bring about (and still is!) in the lives of people.

It is possible to look to psychology for the answers to our relationship difficulties. It will provide a valid and helpful framework for developing healthy, open relationships. But it can do little to provide us with God-given love, concern and compassion; the

characteristics so necessary for the good relationships that provide the context for the sharing of Jesus – the giver of abundant life.

Through relationships that portray the qualities discussed in this chapter, we, as Christians seeking to share the Good News about Christ, can earn the right to speak!

For this to happen most effectively we must:

1. Be consistent in all aspects of our life.

2. Be prepared to share what Jesus means to us in our lives.

3. Be able to communicate the Good News about Jesus and the saga of God's interventions with humanity through history.

Above all, we are to treat others with the integrity and respect they deserve as fellow human beings, the pinnacle of God's creation.

How do we build a strong leadership team?

Leadership is a key issue for youth ministry and ought to be taken seriously by the whole church. It is a team thing, minister, elders, parents being part of the team and discovering who are the appropriate people with the appropriate characteristics and skills to take up the task of leadership.

Choosing your leadership team

1. Choose

Minister, elders, those responsible should take time to look over the jobs and share insights as to who they feel would be the appropriate people with the appropriate gifts for the youth ministry team for a period of one, two or three years.

2. Call

Representatives from that group of ministers and elders should plan to visit those chosen and ask them to consider the leadership responsibility as a call from God through the life of the church.

3. Contract

A contract or description of what the task would involve should be talked about and worked through. Matters needing to be discussed include – assistance in terms of baby sitting, relief for a parent, from a church committee or responsibilities so that the person being called will be fully aware of the task and what it will involve.

4. Commission

Leaders need to be commissioned at the beginning of their leadership period, preferably in an act of worship. Here they have a chance to share with the family of the church the nature of the task and have the church set them aside through prayer and symbolic gestures.

5. Care for them

The church then has the responsibility of caring for its leaders in a range of pastoral and practical ways as the period of the leadership evolves. It is looking to a team and it is taking recruitment seriously.

6. Training leaders

There are a number of methods that need to be taken seriously.

a) The apprentice style method. Having potential leaders work along with current leaders through planning and evaluation meetings building for the future.

b) Leadership retreats. It is appropriate for leaders and potential leaders to have a weekend together or several week nights, planning for the year using a mixture of leadership training sessions along with practical planning for the group.

c) Preparation of Bible study leaders. For short term Bible study programs in youth ministry it is appropriate for the leaders to meet together and actually do the appropriate number of sessions for the study.

If it is a 6 week Lenten study it may be appropriate for the leaders to meet for 6 weeks to actually use the studies that they will then be using with their groups. Have the prospective leaders take it in turns, in pairs, to lead a night and spend time at the end of the night evaluating the effectiveness of the study and the leaders' involvement.

Great things can come from this model as leaders become familiar with the content and learn by doing.

7. The true apprenticeship model

Dave Stone from the United States has developed what may seem to be a simplistic model and yet has great merit. It has four points.

a) *I do it.* I am the only person who can lead this group. I am unsure of potential leaders so I will do it on my own.

b) *I do it – you do it with me.* The group has progressed through a period of 6 months or 1 year and there is someone who has emerged as a leader and it is appropriate that for this period we do it together. We spend time in planning, we share the load and we evaluate.

c) *You do it and I will help.* The prospective leaders have proved themselves and it is time for them to test their wings. We allow them to take major responsibility and we step into the back seat, offering support and back up, feedback and encouragement.

d) *You do it and I will move on to something else.* The leaders have developed to the point where they are capable of running the group and doing it well. My skills can be better used in another situation, but we will be sure to encourage that person to be picking up somebody else and so the discipling will continue.

The importance of a strong leadership team of young people, and adults who are young at heart is an essential part to significant youth ministry. It won't just happen, we have to work hard and plan for it.

Are team dynamics important?

A number of dynamics need to take place amongst the leadership team.

1. Sharing history

It is important for the team to meet together, to share a meal, to go for supper, and get to know each other informally. Leadership teams are encouraged also to build some semi-formal times when they can share something of their life and faith pilgrimage. Then understandings can develop and gifts and areas of skill can be recognised.

2. Pray

Opportunity needs to be made for the team to pray together; to pray for the group, for individuals, for particular aspects of the group's life.

3. Planning and evaluation

Formal opportunities must be made for the group to plan ahead and evaluate events and meetings that have taken place. Opportunities need to be made within these meetings for frank and honest discussion. Take time to talk about the things that have gone well, the things that didn't go so well and why. Use every opportunity to affirm people who have fulfilled tasks and done them well.

It's a great privilege to belong to a team and when the team achieves a particular goal then real Christian fellowship – koinonia – is experienced.

How do I get everything done on time?

Planning to use my leadership time effectively

Time flies!
I haven't got time to prepare!
Time always gets away from me!

These are the often heard cries in youth leadership. Time is a gift from God. We can't accumulate it or store it. The only thing we can do is use it and use it effectively and efficiently.

The following hints may help you get things done on time.

Work out where your time is going now

Keep a record of blocks of time in your week and rate them in terms of being productive, relaxing, wasted.

Work out your time, marking which are the most productive hours in your day and which are least productive.

Try to establish specific times that you could give yourself wholeheartedly to planning and preparing for your task.

Use WORKSHEETS 10 and 11 at the end of this chapter to plan for your week. On 'Things to do today' plan your next day before you go to bed. On the 'Weekly planner sheet' plan your next week perhaps on a Sunday night.

Fill out your work, sporting and social activities. Block in your leadership planning times, and don't forget to plan for your spiritual development time.

Delegate

If you are going to be a good leader you will need to get things done through other people. This will assist your own performance as a leader and it will involve others who can develop their gifts and in some instances do the job better than you can.

Make sure you are giving clear instructions and appropriate authority to the person you are assigning a task. Assure them of your confidence and be willing to let them fail, remembering that you must retain responsibility.

Ed Daynton in his book *Time Management* suggests that you need to be clear on the level of delegation you have made. That may be:

'Do it and don't report back'
'Do it and let me know what you did'
'Tell me what you are going to do but go ahead and do it unless I say otherwise'
'Check all the alternatives and make a recommendation'.

Be prepared to cope with interruptions

Our best planned weeks and days can be completely destroyed by interruptions. These can be things like:
— the telephone
— meetings
— unexpected visitors
— mail
— sickness
— unexpected work commitments.

We can't control interruptions but we can work on them, deal with them positively and not let them get us down.

There are a number of books that could help you if this is a major concern for you.

Learn to say 'NO'

Leaders are not being true to their calling and those whom they are called to lead if they are continually taking on more tasks even with the best of intent.

Learn to say 'no' with grace and fair explanations. This will probably give people more confidence to ask you to do something again when it is appropriate. If you learn to say 'no' with confidence you will probably be better equipped to say 'yes' at appropriate times.

Finish the task on the first go if at all possible

Once you have tackled a particular leadership task or project try and follow it through to the finish. A pile of half finished jobs becomes depressing and frustrating. If a project is too large to complete in one sitting break it into smaller parts and work on those individually.

WORKSHEET 10: Things to do today

Things to do	Priority	Time needed	Done		Schedule
			☐		8:00
			☐		8:30
			☐		9:00
			☐		9:30
			☐		10:00
			☐		10:30
			☐		11:00
			☐		11:30
			☐		12:00
			☐		12:30
			☐		1:00
			☐		1:30
			☐		2:00
			☐		2:30
			☐		3:00
			☐		3:30
			☐		4:00
			☐		4:30
			☐		5:00
			☐		5:50
			☐		6:00
			☐		6:30
			☐		7:00
			☐		7:30
			☐		8:00
			☐		8:30
			☐		9:00
			☐		9:30
			☐		10:00

WORKSHEET 11: Weekly planner sheet

THE WEEK

	SUNDAY	MONDAY	TUESDAY	WEDNESDAY	THURSDAY	FRIDAY	SATURDAY
MORNING							
AFTERNOON							
EVENING							

GOALS FOR THIS WEEK

1 ....
....
2 ....
....
3 ....
....
4 ....
....
5 ....
....

PREPARATION TIME TO SCHEDULE

1 ....
....
2 ....
....
3 ....
....
4 ....
....
5 ....
....

Chapter 5

Making groups work

Making groups work

What role do groups play?	59
How do we develop a friendly caring group?	60
How do we bring out the best in each other?	62
How does the leader function?	63
How do we give good up front leadership?	65
How do we deal with difficult young people?	67
How do we help our group reach out?	68
WORKSHEET 12: How caring is your group?	70
WORKSHEET 13: Four ways to grow a group	71
WORKSHEET 14: Survival – a simulation game	72

What role do groups play?

Groups play an important role in the development and growth of young people and youth ministry within the life of the church.

Young people are both similar and different. Within any one group, kids will have different needs that vary from week to week, month to month. They join groups or clubs for a range of different reasons:

- boredom and frustration
- a desire for companionship (own & opposite sex)
- as a sign of independence, freedom from the family, freedom from authoritarian direction
- conformity – their friends or people they admire go along
- opportunities for peer approval
- leadership opportunities
- chance to do things they are not allowed to do or not able to do alone or without supervision.

Purpose of a group

If asked to declare the function of a group young people would probably respond and say 'That's our Friday night social group' or 'a Wednesday night Bible study group' or 'a Sunday morning sharing group' or 'that's a discipleship growth group'.

These are the specific titles of a group but there are other functions that operate that young people may never identify, recognise or verbalise. Nevertheless these functions are happening.

Functions of a group

Friend-finding

Activities in youth group programs can allow people to mix, as well as provide free time where participants can informally talk together.

Independence practice

Young people welcome opportunities to prove to themselves and others that they can stand on their own feet. Leaders should ensure that they are given maximum possible opportunity to exercise independence. Young people may be hostile to leaders who always tell them what to do.

Safe socialising

Young people who want to be part of a group may find that some non-church groups are hostile to many of the values of their parents. In church youth groups they can enjoy the pleasures of being in a peer group as well as having some kind of responsible leadership to fall back on. With responsible leaders around, you can ensure that aggression won't get out of hand and young people have less risk of being pressured into doing things that will cause conflict with parents.

Substitute parent figures

Adult leaders may take on some of the qualities and roles of a father or mother. For many kids, home is an unhappy place where open, warm communication with parents is lacking. For these young people, the youth group may provide the arena for meaningful relationships with older leaders. However, as their needs changes, the young people will probably move onto other relationships. This change is not necessarily a reflection on the leader, but is often a sign of a job well done.

Recreation

Youth groups may be a place to find or have access to recreational equipment not normally available to the young person. This applies especially in poorer areas, where the lure of good recreational equipment may be a strong basis of attraction to a group.

Extended range and variety of experiences –

for example camping, art, craft, first aid, hobbies, educational films, group discussion, etc.

Practice of social skills

Young people can develop skills in being at ease with new people and the opposite sex, engaging in conversation, dancing.

They can be provided with opportunity to learn how to be a chairperson, act as a secretary and take part in orderly discussions.

They can learn how to get things done; call workers together, direct and organise a committee, arrange entertainment details, make purchases.

This highlights the need for young people to play a major role in planning and developing programs and projects.

How do we develop a friendly caring group?

The leadership team has an important role to play to help the group develop skills in friendship and caring that will enable it to be open and attractive and thus allow participants to experience something of real Christian community. This won't happen without process and content being worked on by the leadership team

Process

Lyman Coleman has developed what we know as the Serendipity Approach which illustrates steps in a process towards achieving community.

Serendipity

Horace Walpole coined the word 'serendipity' in 1754 to mean 'the facility of making happy chance discoveries'. And this is what a Serendipity group is all about – a family of like-minded strugglers making happy chance discoveries together.

Most people use about 10% of their potential. The remaining 90% is buried underneath a pile of fears, failures, painful childhood memories, broken dreams, mistakes and guilt feelings. With such baggage, it's hard to feel O.K.

This is where a Serendipity group comes in. In the company of sympathetic, caring, loving people, we are able to open up and talk about our hangups and fears as well as our hopes and dreams for the future. Instead of getting negative feedback from others, we get positive feedback – affirmation. I affirm you in this venture... I affirm this gift... I affirm this task in your life... Slowly, the affirmation from those we have come to love and trust overcomes the negative feelings we have fed into our computers over the years... and we are able to say, 'I am worthwhile... I have unique gifts... I can accomplish the thing... I will try again...'

History giving

This kind of group doesn't just happen. It is the result of a conscious and purposeful effort. And it takes time to become a real depth support community. To understand this process, picture a baseball diamond. Home plate in the ball diamond is the depth support community – the goal we are seeking. In the New Testament, the word 'koinonia' is used to describe it – a marriage-like relationship in which you can be totally open and free to share your pain and sorrow, hopes and dreams – without fear of condemnation – and to support one another in perfect love.

To get to home plate, however, you must go around the bases together. First base might be called history-giving. Here, as group participants, you need to take time to tell about yourselves:
a) Your past; where you came from; your background; your family relationships, with the good times and bad times; your childhood dreams; your religious roots; and how all of this contributed to the person you are right now.
b) Your present; where you are on your pilgrimage right now; your job; your hobbies; concerns, and where you need to go from here.

c) Your future; where you want to be five years from now; the scary thing you want to try; what you feel God is calling you to be and do.

It takes a long time for each person to give this kind of information, but it is absolutely crucial if the group is going to be a real support community. The more you know about one another, the more you can love one another, because love is the outgrowth of knowledge and understanding.

Affirmation

After two or three sessions of history-giving, you need to move on to second base, which might be called feedback. Here you get a chance to respond to each other, to tell what you have observed and discovered about one another during your time together.

Affirmation is the approach that Jesus often used in his ministry. For instance, with Simon he said, 'Simon, you shall be called Peter, a rock' (Matthew 16:15-19). And with Zacchaeus he said, 'Be quick and come down; I must come and stay with you today... for this man too is a son of Abraham' (Luke 19:1-9). Affirmation is the process of recognising in other people positive strengths, gifts, values and abilities – and the potential – that they cannot see in themselves.

Goal setting

Now, as a group, you are ready to move to a new level of group involvement, which is called goal-setting (third base on the ball diamond). In the atmosphere of a love that is a natural outgrowth of affirmation, you are given the opportunity to say where you need to grow, where you need to 'step out of the boat' in the next risky adventure of your life, what God is calling you to do or be.

This kind of disclosure would have been very risky in the first sessions. However, when you have established a level of trust and confidence with one another it is only natural to share these things. In fact, to keep this kind of information from the others would be robbing the group of its basic purpose for existence – to become a supportive, healing community in which the Holy Spirit ministers to you through the gifts God has distributed among the people 'or the building up of the Body of Christ'.

Koinonia

Now you can reach home plate – 'koinonia' – or depth support community. It is Jesus Christ who makes this unity possible through his Spirit.

There is no need for communication exercises or structured group designs here, because the facilitation of the group has shifted from outside control to a mysterious new control system. The Spirit is free to move in and through the people in the group.

When you reach this point, you will know it. And until you have experienced it, there is no way to explain it. Maybe the closest description might be the phrase – 'a spiritual marriage'. There are many practical exercises and strategies that can open up the four bases of the diamond. See Recommended Reading for books of ideas and exercises to help group building.

Content

There are three ingredients to a vital group:
  1) personal growth
  2) group building
  3) task or mission.

These three functions are like the legs of a stool. Try to do without any one of the three and the whole thing collapses.

1. Personal growth

Personal growth has to do with discovering yourself as a person – your unique gifts, strengths and weaknesses; your spiritual and intellectual formation; coming to terms with yourself as an individual; being a 'whole' person.

2. Group building

Group building has to do with becoming a team – a community of love, trust and acceptance where you feel part of each other and can minister to each other as the body of Christ; to discover the meaning of 'koinonia'. But let us note something right here. A GROUP DOES NOT BECOME A GROUP MERELY BY SITTING DOWN TOGETHER. It takes time to become a group – and it takes caring, sharing, forgiving and affirming – just like marriage.

3. Task or mission

Task or mission has to do with taking responsible action, individually and collectively, to share your life with others. This can be anything from a weekend lay-witness mission to an involvement in race relations, but it should grow out of your life together.

A happy balance

The trick is to keep all three of these emphases in perspective.

Unfortunately, some groups emphasise one of the ingredients to the total exclusion of the others. For instance, one group may spend all its time in study and prayer and end up with spiritual indigestion – while another group may spend all its time sitting around trying to figure out what to do about poverty and end up spiritually bankrupt.

One possible solution to this problem is to assign an equal amount of time at every session to each emphasis:
a) 20 minutes to personal growth and study
b) 20 minutes to group building and sharing
c) 20 minutes to task discussion and prayer.

This might be called a static view of group flow. It will give a group balance, but may force it into study and mission before it has become an established group.

A second possibility is to recognise the priority of 'group building' and spend the largest

amount of time at the beginning of any new or fragmented group on group building. Then, once the group has learned to work as a team, spend less and less time on group building and more and more time on personal growth and mission. This view might be called the dynamic view of group flow.

Both views have their advantages. However, if the group has agreed to meet for several weeks together (or longer), the second view has a better chance for more significant results.

How do we bring out the best in each other?

To call forth the best in each other is the goal of youth groups – but unfortunately few groups know how to do this.

The purpose of the group is to help each one in it to reach full potential. This is a game where everyone must win – everyone must come out on top.

And the way this is done is called enabling. The word enable means to pull from, to call forth, to allow to emerge, to realise the potential of. This is what a youth group is all about.

All of us yearn for fellowship where we can feel a oneness that calls forth the best in each other; to minister to one another as the Body of Christ. Before this can happen, however, we must run the risk of being known – and this is scary. We are afraid that if people find out who we are inside they will reject us. So, to cover up the real person inside, we talk about the weather, about football, about the latest joke in town. And all the while, down deep inside, we are crying out for love.

But love is the result of knowledge, and knowledge comes when we are willing to let another person know us as we really are.

One of the best ways to bring a group to face their level of commitment to each other is to ask them to evaluate their experiences according to three levels of sharing:

1. mouth to mouth
2. head to head
3. heart to heart.

The mouth to mouth sharing is simply conversational doodling – the weather, football, etc.

The head to head sharing is more serious in that it is exchanging ideas and concepts – but the exchange is strictly as ideas detached from the persons.

The heart to heart sharing, on the other hand, lets the other person know where you stand in relation to ideas and how you feel about them on the inside. The heart to heart sharing might be referred to as communing... and communing is the stuff from which community is born.

A group can very easily sit and play verbal volleyball with each other, and this is okay. But don't expect real Christian community in this atmosphere. Community happens when one person dares to say, 'This is the way I feel... In all honesty, this is where I am... This is me... see me... know me... I want to be a part of you and I want you to be a part of me... I want you to know me... I want to know you – deeply'. When this starts to happen in a group, watch out!

'The inner life of many people is simply vacant. They may have once had a faith to give life coherence and meaning, but the widespread materialism around them and the corrosions of secularistic philosophy in education have robbed them of it. So we fill our hands and our time with all kinds of activity to make us forget, while our souls are empty of those convictions and standards which alone give life purpose and direction. People turn to pleasure, business, radio and television, sex, drink, drugs – anything to fill the emptiness within.

LIVING IS LOVING
LOVING IS KNOWING
KNOWING IS RISKING'

Sam Shoemaker

How does the leader function?

Enabling the group to develop

The leader has two major areas of responsibility in terms of enabling a group to develop, maintain itself and grow. These are often referred to as:
- task functions which must be carried out to achieve the defined goal or goals
- and maintenance functions which strengthen and maintain the group as it exists.

It is a little like developing performance skills for football or basketball and also maintaining team spirit and co-operation to provide a sense of satisfaction and achievement for those who are members of the team.

Task functions

Initiating activity

Proposing solutions, suggesting new ideas, new definitions of the problem, new attacks on problems or new organisation of material, for example, 'Why don't we...'

Information seeking

Asking for clarification of suggestions, requesting additional information or facts, for example, 'Does anyone know the cost...'

Information giving

Offering facts in generalisations, relating one's own experience to group problems, to illustrate points, for example, 'It costs $8.00.'

Opinion giving

Stating an opinion or belief concerning a suggestion or one of several suggestions, particularly concerning its value rather than its factual basis, for example, 'I believe indoors is better because...'

Elaborating

Clarifying, giving examples or developing meanings, trying to envision how a proposal might work out if adopted, for example, 'It seems to me that we are saying...'

Co-ordinating

Showing relationships among various ideas or suggestions, trying to pull ideas and suggestions together, trying to draw together activities of various sub-groups or individuals, for example, 'I think Sue and Harry are really saying the same thing in different ways.'

Maintenance functions

Encouraging

Being friendly, warm, responsive to others, praising others and their ideas, agreeing with and accepting contributions of others, for example, 'That's a good idea Sue; let's hear it again.'

Gate-keeping

Trying to make it possible for another person to make a contribution to the group by saying, 'We haven't heard anything from Jim yet', or suggesting limited talking time for everyone so that all will have a chance to be heard.

Standard setting

Expressing standards for the group to use in choosing its content or procedures or in evaluating its decisions. Reminding the group to avoid decisions which conflict with group standards, for example, 'If we all talk at once, we'll never reach a decision'.

Following

Going along with decisions of the group, somewhat passively accepting ideas of others, serving as audience during group discussion and decision making, for example, 'I have nothing to add. It seems a good idea to me.'

Expressing group feeling

Summarising what group feeling is sensed to be, describing reactions of the group to ideas or solutions, for example, 'What you seem to be saying is...'

Evaluating

Submitting group decisions or accomplishments to comparison with group standards, measuring accomplishments against goals, for example, 'Is that really consistent with worship?'

Consensus testing

Tentatively asking for group opinions in order to find out if the group is nearing consensus on a decision, sending up trial balloons to test group opinions, for example, 'Do you all agree?'

Harmonising

Mediating, conciliating differences in points of view, making compromise solutions, for example, 'Perhaps fortnightly might be a good way to start...'

Tension reducing

Draining off negative feelings by jesting or pouring oil on troubled waters, putting a tense situation in wider context, for example, 'I can see the reaction of the ladies in the choir already...'

Leadership styles

Leaders will need to develop skills and styles which will enable them to provide the maintenance and task functions and relate to the group and individuals within the group through a whole range of experiences.

The following diagram suggests three major leadership styles that would operate in groups.

Whilst we would seek most often to operate in the democratic model, there are times when it is appropriate for the other two models to be used and leaders need to develop sensitivity and understanding in when it is appropriate to move from model to model.

LEADERSHIP STYLES

	AUTHORITARIAN (Autocratic)	LAISSEZ-FAIRE (Permissive)	DEMOCRATIC (Shared) (Group centred)
Observed behaviour	Lines of communication run from leader to individual members. *Group* is directed by the leader. *Members* are dependent on him/her.	Lines of communication run in sub-groups, with little link to leader or other sub-groups. *Group* is fragmented, lacks direction. *Members* are independent.	Lines of communication *flow* within the circle. *Group* plans and acts together. Members are inter-dependent.
Underlying Leadership Attitude	Authoritarian OR Autocratic	Laissez-faire OR Permissive	Group-centred OR Enabling
Leadership Pattern	"He/she is the leader"	"He/she is not a good leader"	"We all share in leadership"
Decision Making Pattern	"He/she makes the decisions or he/she allows us to decide by vote."	"We don't seem able to make decisions."	"We all share in making decisions after a *full* and *open* discussion."
Sense of Membership Responsibility	"I *may* share in the group but I am not ultimately responsible."	"I *may* share in the group but I don't need to be responsible."	"I, in co-operation with the others, am ultimately responsible."
Degree of Member Interest	"Why do I have to do this?"	"What's the use of coming here?"	"I'm glad I can take part."

How do we give good up-front leadership?

Leaders will have many opportunities for doing up-front work:
- announcements
- introducing activities
- leading devotions
- involving kids in group work
- etc...!

Leaders can learn more about effective up-front work. Some find it easier than others. However by concentrating, preparing well, and taking time over your presentation an effective job can be done.

Always work out – how you will start – how you will conclude.
In your presentation:

Tell 'em what you're going to tell 'em	: Intro
Tell it to 'em	: Guts
Tell 'em what you told 'em	: Conclusion

A checklist for up-front work

* Gain silence and attention of the group.
* Clear concise delivery.
* Make sure you can see the whole group and vice-versa.
* Set a good climate so the group will be receptive to what you are saying.
* Have a good position in relationship to the rest of the group.
* Be enthusiastic about what you're saying.
* Gauge the length of time of presentation.
* Prefer note form – use key sentences to remind you of points to make.
* Show emotions where appropriate.
* Use eye contact and body language.
* Have sufficient volume for all to hear.
* Know what you are talking about.
* Use visual aids where possible.
* Talk to the level of the group – use appropriate terminology.
* Be prepared to make changes in presentation.
* Talk with an interesting voice.
* Don't fidget or use continuous mannerisms.
* Share input to group, have breaks in input where appropriate.
* Give opportunity for constructive feedback.
* Try to perceive how the group is acting and reacting to your presentation.
* Dress appropriately – wear clothes that will enhance what you are trying to communicate.

N.B. To accomplish all the points in this checklist would mean that a 'super up-fronter' had been created – they are merely helpful points to 'strive' for in doing up-front work. Needless to say, different points would have to be emphasised for different up-front situations, e.g. different points would be emphasised for leading a recreation as compared to leading a worship.

Gain the opinion of others

Check out, with those you respect about how you feel and how they feel you went with your up-front presentation. Sharing like this with constructive criticism and care can be one of the best methods for developing your up-front work.

Preparation for up-front work

Different levels of preparation

a) Write it out word for word
- underline parts to be emphasised
- leave spaces for pauses
- think about the meaning of what you are going to say so that you give it meaningful expression.

b) Write out your introduction and conclusion, list the main points to be covered with a few sub-points – examples etc.

c) List the main points and introduction.

d) Think through the main points and introduction.

When are the different levels appropriate?

It depends on:
how big the occasion is
the impact required
your experience
your self-confidence
the formality of the occasion.

When doing up-front work:

be heard	absolutely essential
be seen	very important
be cheerful	(unless disciplining)

be enthusiastic/alive/expressive.

Useful points checklist:
dress appropriately
use resources – O.H.P., newsprint, puppets
remove barriers
use confident, friendly body language
use humour
Evaluate your up-front work
Think about how it 'felt' and why – what went well, went badly, why? Ask for feedback from

people you respect who will be honest. Reflect on that feedback.

Climate setting

(Please note: Climate setting is jargon for getting people in the right mood).

Setting the climate for a meeting will make an incredible difference. Just as there are good examples of climate setting there are also bad ones and many will come to mind.

When thinking about setting the climate, leaders need to take into account the shape and space of the room or hall, the attitude and the preparation that would be expected of the leaders and some initial activities that will get young people involved and on the appropriate wavelength.

Often singing, tape music, lighting, decorations, posters on walls, chairs set out, cushions provided are things that put a group into the appropriate climate for a specific meeting or event. The following climate setting ideas will be of help to leaders.

Climate setting ideas

Physical activities

Rowdy:
  Bright lighting
  Have equipment ready – balls etc.
  Incentive
  Decor for dancing
  Activities e.g. music happening when people arrive
  Fun callisthenics
  Physical jerks
  Music and singing. Move from rowdy to quieter
Quieter:
  Have equipment set up beforehand
  Quiet background music
  Appropriate location
  Prayer
  Songs.

Discussion/study nights

Provide positions so that everyone can see each other.
Blow off steam before 'study'
Share an ice breaker
Move from larger group to small groups when appropriate.
Have some input 'thought provoker':
  — slides
  — music
  — quiz etc.
  — posters
  — video
Make the physical environment a comfortable trusting atmosphere
Songs
Prayer.

Worship/devotion

Share aims and expectations
Physical arrangement – make it a warm atmosphere
Use a different room, sit on large carpet square, cushions, bean bags

Have supper between activity – devotion
Dim-light technique for meditation
Use appropriate voice

End of night	— devotion becomes an act of sending out
Songs	— appropriate to the theme
Prayers	— topics from the group — pray in pairs or in fours — just the leader leading praying

Meetings, planning, committees

Prepared chairperson and secretary
Prepared agenda – open for other topics
Room set out
Ten minute gossip time – share how your week has been
Prayer – use prayer time for specifics from the meeting or from Individual concerns
Pray in pairs.

How do we deal with difficult young people?

Kids can be difficult. Most kids will be difficult at different times, some kids will be difficult more often than others. It is very easy for the leader to 'freak out', give a kid a mouth full. It is much more difficult to try and get behind the reason for the difficulty and to provide an objective and helpful possibility for that young person to fit into the life of the group.

Discipline

Discipline is a word that has slipped from the life of the church for a wide range of reasons. It is a word closely associated with the word 'disciple' which means being a learner. A leader will need to have some discipline.
Quotable quotes:

'A good leader/teacher has good discipline.'

'Discipline does not equal punishment.'

'Discipline is aimed at the behaviour, punishment is aimed at the person.'

'Discipline helps set the tone and creates the atmosphere for a group.'

'Discipline is more than securing obedience.'

Biblical views on discipline

1. God shows loving care for all people by showing them the need to be disciplined. God urges parents to give discipline for the sake of their children.
Hebrews 12:5-11
Ephesians 6:1-4

2. There are times for righteous and just anger which will be seen by the angry parents' actions.

In the time of Moses (wilderness). Amongst the prophets (for the people).
Jesus – Luke 6:6-11
Luke 19:45-48

3. God's love however, is always fair and just, and so should our discipline be fair and just.
Ephesians 4:26
Colossians 3:21

4. It is unchristian to punish in a spirit of revenge.
Matthew 5:43-48

Good communication dissolves many potential behavioural problems. Two ways of achieving this are active listening and 'I' messages.

Active Listening – listening for the underlying feeling and responding to it rather than simply to the spoken word, for example, a student says 'I'm fed up with this silly lesson. It can't be proved and it doesn't help us'. The teacher responds with 'You feel frustrated and this lesson isn't answering your questions'.

By responding with roadblocks such as threatening words, lecturing, judging, name calling, we block further communication.

'I' Messages – to communicate your feelings and problems you have with a person's behaviour. 'When several people call out at once I feel quite frustrated (feeling owned), because I won't be able to hear your answers and nor will the people in the class.' (Tangible results of the behaviour giving rise to the feeling.)

Know your young people

A good leader will get to know the young people in the group. The leader will be familiar with names, hobbies, interests, musical tastes, football allegiance – the things that will provide conversation beyond 'hello, how are you'.

As the leader gets to know individuals, opportunities can be taken to work with problem kids in terms of giving them a task to do, spending quality time with them, matching them up with other kids who will bring out the best in them and so on.

The leader will want to 'minister' to all the group and particularly to problem kids with the hope and goal that eventually the group will minister to each other as a Christian community. When one person takes the leap and decides to let the others in on his or her life, the group is under a real obligation as the Body of Christ to be the ministering servants to this person.

The following four hints will assist the growth of that sense of community.

1. **Don't interrupt.** Keep your mouth shut – and let the person talk. The chances are that no one has ever really listened before. The greatest thing we can offer is our ears. Many times this is all a person needs – and wants. Remember, the greatest counsellors say the least.

This may mean dispensing with the agenda for that session and giving over the entire time to a person who needs to share feelings and hurting on the inside. After all, the purpose of the group is to enable each other, not to cover the agenda. The leader of the group should be sensitive at this point and be prepared to adjust the schedule. Ask, 'Have you said all that you have to say about this?' or 'Would you like to add anything before we go on?' or 'Are you trying to tell us something?' These questions are enabling questions that let a person go a little deeper in his or her sharing.

2. **Don't probe.** There is a thin line between listening and probing, but it is a very important one. To listen is to enable a person to say all there is to say. To probe is to make a person share what should not be revealed at that time. A probing question takes the initiative away from the person who is sharing – and this is bad.

If someone in the group starts to probe, the leader should step in immediately with 'Let Bill tell it the way he sees it' or 'Why don't we give Rose a chance to finish what she has to say?'

3. **Don't give advice.** The cheapest thing in the world is advice. Very often, the person with the least information is the most free with advice – and the results are disastrous. If someone in the group has had a similar experience, that person can share the experience – without telling the other person what to do.

If someone in the group starts to give advice, the leader should break in immediately and say, 'Why don't you share your experience but let Helen make her own application?' or 'Let's hold off on the advice and stick just to our own experience!'

4. **Don't judge.** If the group really is one, some sensitive areas of disagreement in lifestyle, theology and outlook are going to come up. Here is the place where love is going to be put to the test. When you violently disagree with others, can you give them the right to their own viewpoint? Can you simply affirm them, and release them to be themselves, to think as they must? This does not mean giving in or making concessions. This means saying, 'I cannot see it the way you see it... but I love you and accept you just as you are and with what you believe'.

When this kind of listening, caring, loving, accepting thing happens in a group, you will know it... and so will everyone else. This is what it is all about.

Remember, 'to enable' is to call forth the best in others, to see the best in them, to affirm the best in them. Are you an enabler?

How do we help our group to reach out?

This particular question is covered in far more detail in Chapter 11 'Evangelism'.

The group if it is to grow will need to reach out in a number of ways.

To each other

Many groups are stifled by subgroups that only communicate with each other. We need first and foremost to encourage and develop opportunities for kids within the group to get to know each other and feel free to relate across the group through fun, sensitivity, caring and sometimes prayer.

Within the life of the church

The group needs to see its place within the total life of the local church. Many opportunities exist for the group to make contributions to the overall family through involvement in worship, the church concert, the annual fete or street stall, a special mission activity. The implications are most important as young people will discover that they are part of the larger family of the church and can find acceptance and friendship with people of all ages.

Beyond their local scene

Kids in local groups need the opportunity from time to time to come out of their small cabbage patch and see themselves as part of the wider scene of the church. This needs to happen within a particular denomination and at an ecumenical level as well. The chance to attend a presbytery or regional Easter camp, a state camp or rally, a national youth convention or an international gathering of Christians, is a significant milestone in faith development as young people see that the Christian world is broader and often richer than they have known. Reaching out in this way enables a transition to be smoother when young people have to leave home for study, travel, or vocation.

Reaching out to kids in their neighbourhood

Young people in local groups need to be inspired and educated to see the task of evangelism and outreach as their role, as part of their response to the claims of Christ in their lives. The opportunity to reach out and invite others in, first to the friendship of the group and then into the fellowship of the Christian faith should be basic in our thinking and our acting.

WORKSHEETS 12, 13 and 14 will help groups have a good look at themselves so that they may be better equipped to reach out and bring others in.

WORKSHEET 12: How caring is your group?

YES NO

1. Does my group encourage new people? ☐ ☐

2. Are new people formally introduced? ☐ ☐

3. Is there a person or group of people assigned to help get a newcomer acquainted? ☐ ☐

4. If a person is sick does the group send a card ☐ ☐

5. Did my group increase its numbers last year? ☐ ☐

6. Is new leadership elected regularly? ☐ ☐

7. If someone is missing does this cause concern and is there a follow-up? ☐ ☐

8. Does the leadership meet regularly to plan? ☐ ☐

9. Do we have a project that goes outside the parish? ☐ ☐

10. Do we have social activities? ☐ ☐

11. Do we keep a balance between devotional, educational, social activities? ☐ ☐

12. Do we hear regular evaluation? ☐ ☐

13. Is there a communication process by which equal participation is possible in our group? ☐ ☐

14. If I were a total stranger, would I feel accepted by or at home with the group? ☐ ☐

15. Does my group have a way of bringing people on the fringes into active participation? ☐ ☐

16. Does my group have ways to help people deepen their spiritual lives? ☐ ☐

17. Does the group have a way of bringing out and dealing creatively with conflict? ☐ ☐

18. Does the group bring in outside help when it has difficulties? ☐ ☐

19. Does participation in my group promote an individual's participation in the liturgical life of the parish? ☐ ☐

WORKSHEET 13: Four ways to grow a group

1. In small groups of 3 or 4...

List the 5 most popular activities your youth group
has held in the last year and then try to work out why
they were successful.

Activity	Why successful (what kind of success)
i)	
ii)	
iii)	
iv)	
v)	

2. Divide these readings among your groups.
Acts 4:31-34
Matthew 4:17-20
Matthew 14:20 (then look back to 14-20)
Ephesians 4:1-7, 10-13

What do these passages tell us about being in
a Christian group?

3. Come together and share your discoveries in 1. and 2.

4. Individually, write down what you think are the 3 most important things that help a Christian group work.

1. ....

2. ....

3. ....

As a group, using these individual statements,
make up your own list of ' Ways to Grow a Group'.

WORKSHEET 14: Survival

"Survival" by Colin Ray
Copyright – Used with permission

'Survival' is a simulation game that enables participants of a group or potential leaders to look at the qualities of leadership they have found important in terms of planning for future leaders and understanding the role of leadership.

Survival – the scene

A group of thirty 12-15 year olds are going to be isolated on a small island in the Pacific. It has no modern facilities. The island is totally isolated and uninhabited.

Three leaders have to be selected, from the list of 11 candidates described below, to go with these young people to help them begin a new civilisation together. Participants in the game choose their three leaders and put them on the individual rating scale.

1. Small groups of four work together for five minutes only and come to a consensus on the three leaders they would choose.

2. The whole group comes together, the enabler sits back and allows the group to finally choose three leaders.

The enabler should carefully monitor the process of the group and reflect back to the group some of the dynamics that took place.

3. Once the decision has been made on the three leaders, then positive and negative factors should be listed.

Candidates for leadership

MS A. Leads a junior youth group at a local church. She is pretty, bright and happy. She hasn't been a leader for long, but when she is with the group there is a bubbling enthusiasm that seems to go along with her. She works hard at the group, but sometimes feels inadequate for the task. However, each week's encounter with the group shows her something of their potential and promise and encourages her to do her best.

MR B. Mr. B. is leader of a scout group. He is an older man, but a person who has endeavoured always to prepare his program. He prepares himself as well as the program. He doesn't have a lot of skills scholastically, but he is one of whom his group regularly say with pride 'He's my leader!'

MR C. Has been a counsellor for a youth group in the town for some time. In the past, he found things quite easy and when he looked at his group he would notice them neatly dressed, hair done, etc. However, he is finding things somewhat confusing these days. When looking at his group now, he sees a number with very long hair, dressed in jeans and on occasions even coming barefooted. Whenever subjects such as religion, sex and politics are mentioned, he is polite, but quick to change the topic.

MR D. Is a stalwart in the community and a valued member in Rotary. For years he has been the guiding light of the town Rotaract Club. In the town he has many contacts but he can't always be present and even on occasions has been known to forget to turn up altogether.

MS E. Is a physical education instructor at the local High School who also trains two local basketball teams. A rigid disciplinarian, MS. E.'s teams always win, which brings little comfort to parents who see their children constantly agitated lest they lose. She also puts practices on Sunday mornings which concerns some parents whose children have a clash with worship and Sunday school programs.

MR F. Trains a local junior soccer team. He works on the principle that all boys are very much alike, and takes an interest in the boys by using every opportunity to discuss cricket, cars, marbles, etc. The boys think he's beaut even though they know very few rules of soccer, and only win games on forfeit.

MR G. Runs the local Gymnastic Club. He believes that fitness of body and mind are essential to a well-balanced childhood. Thus long periods are spent perfecting technique. Unfortunately, as poor achievers usually receive little commendation, they usually drop out and the group has become a small elite.

How to work with young people. 1991 The Joint Board of Christian Education.

MS H. Runs a guide group. She believes that guiding provides the perfect remedy to all the ills of youth, and that any girl who is a guide, and who assiduously attains her awards could not but help prove to be a balanced citizen of the realm. She spends a considerable time each day checking uniforms and eulogising her girls, thus leaving little time for program. She finds it hard to understand why many girls in her group seem to lose interest and leave.

REV. I. Is a young radical pastor who, against the best guidance of the aging congregation, had the senior youth group lease an old bakehouse and turn it into a coffee-shop, open each night of the week. Kids drop in any time and are encouraged to display any art or pottery they've created. The place occasionally gets a bit out of hand, and there is pressure from solid citizens to close it down. The good Rev. I. also has a tendency to be tough on kids who drink and even seems to hope all who enter will end up 'saved'.

MS J. Runs a girl's group at the local Y.M.C.A. She believes in participation and her whole program is geared toward involvement. She prepares well ahead and provides a varied program. She invites in speakers as well as taking the group out regularly. However, she spends so much time with the group that her husband and family are beginning to complain.

MS K. Runs a church youth fellowship group. She likes young people and looks forward to the time she spends with them each Friday night. Within her group are some stirrers who feel obliged to contradict all she says. When a matter comes up for question she encourages others to give an answer as well. For example, last Friday, one boy questioned the value of worship. MS K. invited the class to answer and then included the following comments in her answer: 'I admit I also sometimes wonder what is achieved by attending worship, but I do attend and I'll tell you why ...'

INDIVIDUAL RATING

1. ....

2. ....

3. ....

SMALL GROUP RATING

1. ....

2. ....

3. ....

Positive factors in leadership

A. ....

B. ....

C. ....

D. ....

E. ....

F. ....

G. ....

H. ....

I. ....

J. ....

K. ....

Negative factors in leadership

A. ....

B. ....

C. ....

D. ....

E. ....

F. ....

G. ....

H. ....

I. ....

J. ....

K. ....

How to work with young people. 1991 The Joint Board of Christian Education.

JESUS' STYLE OF LEADERSHIP

1.

Christian Leader

....

....

....

....

....

....

....

....

....

....

Identify and write down ten (10) things you think a Christian leader should have:

Jesus

....

....

....

....

....

....

....

....

....

....

2. In the column beside that, list down any additional leadership qualities that you see Jesus as having.

3. Having identified Christian leadership qualities in general and some about Jesus, now look at the Bible passages below and identify the leadership qualities about Jesus that you feel the passages show you:

    Mark 3: 13-19..

    Mark 11: 15-17..

    Mark 14: 32-36, 39..

    John 10: 11-16..

    John 13: 2-5..

    John 17: 15-21..

    John 19: 1-11..

    Philippians 2: 5-9..

    ....

4. Now share the above in your small group, in turn, and reflect on what the others have written.

5. Then, complete this sentence:
    'From my own Bible study and our group sharing, I have learnt the following about Jesus' style of leadership ...'

    ....

    ....

    ....

    ....

6. Reflect upon what others see about Jesus' style of leadership in the above Bible passages.

7. Two things I would like to model from Jesus' style of leadership are:
    i) ....

    ii) ....

8. Finally, complete this sentence:
    'To do something about them I will ...'

    ....

How to work with young people. 1991 The Joint Board of Christian Education.

74

Chapter 6

Communicating and caring

Communicating and caring

How do we develop growing friendships with young people?   77

How do I get young people to talk to me?   78

How do we help young people with problems?   79

How do we get along with the parents of young people?   80

How do we help young people follow through faith commitments?   80

WORKSHEET 15: Ways to develop growing friendships   81

WORKSHEET 16: Positive responses   82

WORKSHEET 17: How do we get along with the parents of young people?   83

WORKSHEET 18: Going out - role play   84

WORKSHEET 19: Role play on appearances   85

WORKSHEET 20: Role play on money   86

How do we develop growing friendships with young people?

How do you develop a relationship with anyone?
Friendship is based on
- mutual trust
- honesty
- care, love
- an attraction of minds
- mutual likes
- and many other things.

Young people are open to making friends, no matter how closed they seem in their cliques. They respond well to people in authority treating them as people, rather than as annoying children.

Youth leaders have a perfect opportunity to model good relationships between young people and older people which will reach into the rest of their relationships.

* Ask yourself the question: What things do older people do to me that make me think I am wanted as a friend?

Jesus: a model for pastoral care

The ideal of compassion and concern for others is seen in Jesus of Nazareth. Someone has described Jesus as 'love with skin on it'. At the simplest level, Jesus stands as a reference point within history, indicating to us through his life and teachings the qualities which ought to mark our ministry to others. What are these qualities?

1. Jesus was a man of apparent contradictions. In contrast to popular expectations, Jesus chose for himself the path of a humble servant.

2. Jesus identified with people in their pain and oppression, living a life of poverty with the poor, the outcasts and the unlovely.

3. Jesus saw people not only as they were, but also as they might become.

4. Jesus was more concerned with motives than behaviour.

5. Jesus needed time alone with his Father.

6. Jesus had a concern for healing and forgiveness.

7. Jesus had time for people.

8. Jesus brought hope to people.

9. Jesus allowed people the right to find their own answers and make their own decisions.

10. Jesus listened beyond the words to the real thoughts, feelings and questions at the core of people.

The following accounts of Jesus' interactions with people may confirm or even help you add to the above list.
Luke 19:1-10
John 4:8-30, 39-42
John 8:1-11
John 18:28-40
Matthew 9:2-8
Mark 10:17-22.

How do I get young people to talk to me?

The obvious answer is to listen, but that's not easy! We come from a society of talkers and we have to learn to listen.

10 commandments for active listening

1. Stop talking – simple but very important.

2. Remove distractions – turn off the television, radio, remove the walkman.

3. Concentrate – don't wander off mentally, stay with what is being said.

4. Look interested – nod, make affirming noises to show you are interested.

5. Hear more than words – watch for body language, check that what is being said is what is really meant.

6. Check you are hearing it right – express it in different words,

7. Ask clarifying questions – for example, 'Tell me what you mean by that'.

8. Be patient – wait for it, don't provide the words for the other person.

9. Be non-judgmental – be unshockable, create the impression that what is being said will not colour your opinion of the person.

10. Stop talking – hard task, but necessary.

Sometimes all a person needs is a listener...no advice, wisdom, experience, money assistance, expertise, or even compassion...but just someone to listen, even for a minute or two.

Use WORKSHEET 15 at the end of this chapter to check out ways to develop growing friendships.

GOOD LISTENING INVOLVES
....
....
....
....
....
....
....
....
....
....
....

LISTENING SKILLS I ALREADY USE
....
....
....
....
....
....
....
....
....
....
....
....

LISTENING SKILLS I NEED TO WORK ON
....
....
....
....
....
....
....
....
....

Be trustworthy

Young people need someone they can trust, who considers their conversations confidential. How do you react to the following?

1. Liz (16) tells youth leader Kerry that she is thinking of breaking off her relationship with John (18). Kerry thinks it's going to be hard on John, so she tells Matt, John's best mate.

2. Lisa and Chris (both 16) are having a small fight. Lisa is upset and comes to David (youth leader) for comfort. Two days later Lisa overhears the two other leaders of the youth group laughing at the 'dramas' of teenage relationships.

3. Paul (15) is worried that he is not as physically developed as the guys in the group or at school. He shares his fears with Rob, his youth leader. The next time youth group meets the other boys suggest Paul do some weight lifting, or join a gym.

How do we help young people with problems?

A youth leader is not a psychologist. A youth leader can be a listener, and can sometimes counsel, but often will not have the skill to counsel young people in particular situations.

However, youth leaders can learn to be better listeners and also keep a conversation going until they can recommend someone who has more expertise on the matter. Use WORKSHEET 16 at the end of this chapter. It is an exercise called 'Positive Responses' which is best done in a youth leadership team.

When a young person comes to you, there are varying levels of communication that are used. Below is an example of what happens in a conversation. It is important to understand how people come to disclose their feelings.

Levels of communication

Chit-chat
On a light level, the weather, general talk, setting the scene.

The facts
Delving in to what the issue is – factual, sharing of data, e.g. this happened, at this time, at this place, with these people.

The personal
The feelings, anger, remorse, sadness, laughter.

The moment of truth
What the actual problem is, how it feels, the inescapable truth.

Positive response and levels of how people communicate are good first steps to learn. But how do we help young people with problems?

An important thing to note:

*** You don't have to have all the answers or be a super counsellor. You have to know the people around who have expertise in areas of counselling, so that if necessary, you can go with a young person to get them some professional help. ***

What would you do?

* Merryn comes to you, frightened because Mark has said to her that he feels like committing suicide.
* Sarah and Jason come to you to talk about contraception as they have decided to enter a sexual relationship.
* Fiona, who is usually a bright, bubbly personality, comes to youth group visibly upset and quiet and leaves before you can talk to her.
* Neal is obsessed with war and killing things. He comes to youth group with knives, that he sharpens in front of everybody. He is frightening some of the kids in the group.
* Kathy has just moved from interstate and is angry and bitter that she has had to move with her family. She hates everything about her new life and is in constant conflict with her parents.
* Stephen's father has just died and Stephen is devastated. He bursts into tears in public and spends a lot of time on his own.

There are some things you will feel capable of doing something about in the above situations. However, the best pastoral care of young people is putting them in touch with people who can help them work through issues. This may or may not be you.

How do we get along with the parents of young people?

Use WORKSHEET 17 at the end of this chapter to help you understand how to get along with the parents of the young people in your group.

Another way to help break down the barriers that exist between young people and their parents is to do some intentional exercises, such as role plays.

Three scripted role plays designed to open discussion are WORKSHEETS 18, 19, and 20 at the end of this chapter.

Act out a role play in front of the group.

Break the group up into small groups of five or six and have them go through the questions.

Panel

At the end of the small group time, have the group think of two questions they would ask parents if they had a chance.

With the whole group together, have a panel of 4 or 6 parents.

NOTE: The parents should be unknown to the young people. They should be older, their children grown past their teen years. Try to include at least one single parent.

Each group is given a chance to ask their questions. Open the conversation so that young people feel comfortable asking 'the questions they have always wanted answered, but were afraid to ask!'

How do we help young people follow through faith commitments?

Follow-up is the key to helping young people to help themselves. When young people in your group attend events that may have impact or their faith, it is important that you follow them up
— even if they have made no commitment
— to listen to their impressions and how they felt about the experience.
Important events may include:
— large conventions
— Christian rock concert
— regional and state events
— camps
For those young people who have made significant faith commitments there are some things you can do to help them be faithful to their decision.
— Help them share their experience in a church service.
— Provide pointers for available daily devotional material.
— Encourage them to pick a person or people who will monitor how they are going and support them.
— Talk about what they want to do now and keep them active in that commitment.
— Encourage them to start writing a journal about their faith progress.
— Ask them to think about their life in relation to this new commitment and what they would like to change.
— Pray with and for them.

WORKSHEET 15: Ways to develop growing friendships

Below is a list of ways to develop growing friendships.

Tick (✓) the ones you feel you already do.

Put a cross (x) against ones you don't do.

Put a question mark (?) against ones you feel unsure/doubtful about.

Put an arrow (→) against the ones you will try to do.

Add your own.

- ☐ Visit kids.
- ☐ Find out their interests, hobbies.
- ☐ Resist talking about or asking questions about school.
- ☐ Use humour.
- ☐ Treat them as people, not subjects or objects.
- ☐ Be open, share a bit of yourself (take risks).
- ☐ Share your time.
- ☐ Share your belongings.
- ☐ Follow-up important things in their lives.

- ☐ Attend important events, e.g. concerts, graduations.
- ☐ Invite them to your home.
- ☐ Share meals with them.
- ☐ Listen to them.
- ☐ Be consistent in standards.
- ☐ Don't talk about them to other young people except in a positive way.
- ☐ ....
- ☐ ....
- ☐ ....

WORKSHEET 16: Positive responses

In a group of 3 or 4, nominate one person as reader, one person as responder. The reader reads the first statement on the 'How would you respond?' sheet. The responder says the first thing he or she thinks would be appropriate if this statement were said by a young person.

The rest of the group judges the response:

Thumb up for – 'that was a good response'.
Folded arms for – 'that was okay, but I would have responded a little differently'.
Thumb down for – 'I disagree'.

Then change reader/responder, so that everyone has a turn. Work your way through the sheet.

HOW WOULD YOU RESPOND?

I'm fed up completely with study. I'm going to throw my course in and get a job.

Everybody makes fun of me. No-one likes me. I hate the youth group.

After going out together for a year, my boyfriend has just broken off with me.

It's one thing to have faith in God, when life is neat, but it's not so easy when everything is falling in a heap. It's a pipe-dream to expect God to help. You really have to make it on your own.

Whenever I speak to you, you always agree with everything I say. Why don't you ever offer any opinions of your own?

I don't know what my mates see in boozing on. Last night Glenn was so bad he spewed on the dance floor of the Manhattan. When I suggested we ought to take Glenn home, they abused me and called me a church-going weakie. I know next time I see them they'll be okay with me again, but what am I going to do next time they start getting drunk?

My parents and I just can't get on. We had another fight tonight. I want to move out of home as soon as I can.

I just missed out on another job. No one is ever going to employ me – I might as well give up trying.

I wish I had some friends.

My parents are always fighting – I think they are going to split up.

You've got to help me. Before I went to the party tonight, Dad said, 'If you get home late again tonight, that's it – you won't be coming back into this house'. Well, I was late again, and when I got home I found the house locked and a bag of my clothes on the doorstep. What am I going to do?

My father just died. He was a good man. Why did God let him die?

WORKSHEET 17: How do we get along with the parents of young people?

Below is a check list. Tick the ones you already do and discuss how best to do the ones you don't.

PARENTS OF YOUNG PEOPLE

☐ Visit parents.

☐ Don't play off kids against parents.

☐ Support parents.

☐ Ask parents how they are coping.

☐ Organise your time so that your program finishes when you say it will finish.

☐ Make sure parents know the drop off and pick up times and places.

☐ Make sure parents know where their children will be.

☐ Avoid taking sides with young people against their parents.

☐ Inform parents how their kids are going.

☐ Ask permission to tackle subjects that parents may have problems with you tackling e.g. sex education, drugs.

☐ Ask for their support and help.

☐ Include parents in some of the programs e.g. have a parent/youth dinner.

☐ Care for their young people.

WORKSHEET 18: Going out – role play

Mum, dad, teenage kid. Kid walks in to mum and dad who are standing in lounge room.

K. Umm... can I go to a party at Josie's place?

D. What's it for?

K. *(pause)* I think it's Josie's birthday party.

M. Are her parents going to be home?

D. Is there going to be alcohol?

K. *(quickly)* Oh no, no alcohol, and I'm pretty sure her parents will be there. Can I go?

M. Who else will be there?

K. Everybody!!

D. I think you should ring to check whether her parents are going to be there.

K. *(panicking)* No...! Anyway I don't know her number. Can I go?

M. Were there invitations to this party? Do you have to take a present?

K. Look, I don't know. Can I go?

D. Alright, but we'll pick you up at 12.

K. Are you crazy! Parties only start moving at 11.30, and nobody's parents pick them up.

M. *(angry)* Do you want to go or not?

D. What's wrong with us picking you up? Are you telling the truth? Are the parents going to be home?

K. Look, I didn't expect an inquisition. I only want to go to a party. I'm not going off to join a war or something.

D. Don't use that tone with us or you'll not be going at all.

K. *(frustrated)* Well I may as well not go, having to leave by 12 and getting picked up!

M. That's enough or you won't go. And didn't you go to a party at Josie's once before where people were drunk and almost wrecked the house?

K. Can't I come home at 1.00 or 1.30?

M.&D. No.

K. *(angry)* Just because you go to bed at 9.00 you expect me to be like that. You stifle me. I'm going – but I'm not coming home till 1.30 and I'll walk!

D. You will do as you are bloody well told.

M. Forget the party, you were out last weekend.

K. *(anxious)* Alright, alright. I'll be home by 12. I'll catch a lift with Debbie's parents.

D. Your mother said you can't go and that's the end of it *(walking off)*.

K. Alright, you can pick me up *(chasing parents)*. I'll be home earlier *(parents walk out, kid yells)*. I have to go to this party *(and then screaming)* Aaahhh!

WORKSHEET 19: Role play on appearances

Characters: Mother (M) and Father(F) eating dinner and watching television (football). Young guy (T) going out to party dressed in 'messy' clothes with unusual hair.

Scene: Mum and Dad at table (3/4 view) with plates, knife and fork watching telly (cardboard box), T. walks behind them to an imaginary fridge to get a drink.

M. Are you getting changed soon?

T. I'm changed already.

M. Are you wearing that?

T. Yup.

M. Well haven't you got anything better to wear than those old things? I've bought you stacks of good clothes.

T. For a start, I never asked you to buy them; besides I want to wear these.

M. *(after a pause)* I bought you that nice shirt the other day, why don't you wear that? It's much nicer.

T. Look, I wear what I want, right?

M. Those things don't even match, and they're certainly not appropriate for your cousin's 21st party.

T. How many times do I have to say it, Mother *(loaded with rich sarcasm)*, I wear what I want, and you can't tell me what to do.

M. While you're living in this house young man, not paying board mind you, then you obey a few things we say. You can't go around doing anything you want. Besides, you need a hair cut.

F. Ball!! *(referring to telly, alive and exuberant)*.

T. My hair is my business – no one else's.

M. I pay for it, when it's cut...

T. *(loud)* Just shut up mum!!

M. I beg your pardon!

T. I'm going now, and I'm going like I am whether you like it or not.

M. *(annoyed)* Don't talk to your parents like that...

T. Drop off, I'm going *(walks out)*.

M. *(yells after him)* I think we need to have a talk... *(door slams)*.

M. *(to husband)* Did you hear that? Did you see what he was wearing? *(pause)* What are you going to do?

F. *(suddenly responding)* I reckon shifting Madden to the forward line should do the trick!

WORKSHEET 20: Role play on money

Mum, Dad and teenage kid at dinner table.

K. I have to go into the city to the movies tomorrow. Can I have some money for the train and the film?

D. You're working part-time. Films are what you pay for.

K. No! The money I earn I spend on other things. Everybody else's parents pay for films and stuff like that.

D. We're not everybody else's parents.

M. We can't afford to be giving you money for every little thing you do.

K. You gave Eugene some money for the pictures. You've been buying things like new fridges, video recorders and stuff – you have so got money.

D. Eugene doesn't work – and that was a school thing. You work, if you want to go to the movies you pay.

K. That's not fair.

M. Don't you have any money? You only got paid two days ago.

K. But, I had Shelly's present to buy and I had to pay Colin back, and I bought those jeans.

D. You should have realised when you bought those jeans...

M. *(interrupting)* which you didn't need...

D. ...that you might have wanted money for other things.

K. But I thought you'd pay for this stuff. You did for Eugene.

M. You're always comparing yourself to your younger brother. He needs the money, you don't.

K. *(angry)* Oh that's great! I work my guts out and Eugene doesn't, but I can't get a measly $15.00 for a movie.

M. If you choose to spend your money on useless things like presents for your friends and jeans, that's not our fault.

D. And we've already said! We can't afford to pay for every outing you go on. We'd be in the poor house the amount of times you go out.

K. *(sobbing)* Please, please. I don't have any money at all and I really have to go to this movie, Jason's going. Please?

M. *(sigh)* Alright, this time only, you can have the money.

D. But, we're going to need to sit down with you and budget properly. You're going to have to learn that everything costs.

M. Yes, as I've said...

K. Money doesn't grow on trees?

M.&D. Right!

Chapter 7

Program planning

Program planning

Why do we need groups?   89

How do we plan a good program?   90

How do we know what programs young people
will like?   97

What are some good program ideas?   97

How will people know what's happening with
the group?   98

How do we improve our group?   99

How do we evaluate our programs?   100

WORKSHEET 21: Possible purposes for
friendship and fun groups   101

WORKSHEET 22: An honest look at our group   102

WORKSHEET 23: Sample quarterly program   103

WORKSHEET 24: Sample evening program   104

WORKSHEET 25: Identifying program aims
and objectives   105

WORKSHEET 26: Event planner   106

WORKSHEET 27: Interest finder   107

WORKSHEET 28: Evaluating our youth programs   108

WORKSHEET 29: An evaluation process   109

Why do we need groups?

Groups for young people are an important part of youth ministry, but ministry is much more than groups. The youth group should fulfil specific goals within your parish's overall youth ministry. Our emphasis is on 'fun and friendship' as the basis for any youth group. This strategy recognises that young people need a group in which they feel a sense of belonging and acceptance, and in which they can have fun in a safe, positive environment. The youth group is a place where young people feel comfortable bringing their friends, and in which those friends may have initial contact with the church.

Many churches have youth groups simply because they have always had them, rarely questioning or evaluating the purpose of such groups. In the Uniting Church, it is recommended that parishes provide two sorts of groups for young people:
- A friendship and fun group which has an emphasis on young people getting together for enjoyable activities within the Christian fellowship.
- A discipleship group which has an emphasis on opportunities to explore and discuss issues about faith.

Both these groups should be open to young people who understand the nature of the groups and accept their emphasis and type of program. It will frequently be the case that the friendship and fun group will be larger than the discipleship group.

Young People and Your Church
Action Manual

The Uniting Church in Australia Policy: *Young People and Your Church* makes the following statement about a fellowship and fun group.

A friendship and fun group

A group that starts with friendship and fun and can move towards faith. It will allow 12-14/15 or 15-17/20 year olds to:
- be with others the same age, away from children but not pressured by older teenagers
- do interesting things together
- make friends and have fun
- feel they are welcomed as part of the church
- be involved in some kind of service to others
- be introduced to the good news about Jesus – good news for them and the whole of their lives, for example through studies and devotions, appropriate to the age
- come whether they are Christian or not, where they know they will be welcome even if they don't believe everything the church is on about; but where they can make discoveries, ask honest questions and meet people who put what they believe into practice.

A friendship and fun group will probably be held on an evening. The leaders of this group should also encourage young people to participate in the discipleship group.

WORKSHEET 21, at the end of this chapter, lists some possible purposes for friendship and fun groups.

You could give other leaders WORKSHEET 21 to prioritise, or use it with your youth group.

Being clear about the purpose of the group and its relationship to other activities is the first step in running a dynamic group. Think about your own parish and use WORKSHEET 22, at the end of this chapter, to identify some of the expectations of different people regarding your youth group.

21 keys to effective groups for young people

Groups which are effective in attracting young people and maintaining their involvement and enthusiasm often have a number of common key factors. The list below pushes to the ideal. Your group may show some of these. Hopefully the list will challenge your group to aspire to greater heights.

1. The group has a clear purpose and direction, understood and agreed upon by leaders, group participants, ministers and elders.

2. Young people feel a strong sense of belonging and acceptance from the group and its leaders.

3. The group has a meeting place which it can decorate and call its own.

4. The leaders meet regularly to plan, pray and support each other.

5. The church assigns pastoral elders to the group to care for leaders and participants.

6. The leaders plan the program at least 3 months ahead and involve group participants in planning.

7. The program provides a balance of evenings at the church and away.

8. The program is printed on a 3 monthly basis and distributed to parents and group participants.

9. The leaders visit group participants in their homes regularly.

10. The leaders are well-prepared each week prior to the program commencing.

11. The programs are fun with a good balance of active and passive activities (appropriate to the age group).

12. The group has a regular devotional time which is seen by participants as being relevant and worshipful.

13. The leaders give confident, caring up-front leadership with a consistent approach to discipline.

14. The leaders are enthusiastic, enjoy being with young people, and have a sincere Christian faith.

15. The leaders are willing to get to know individual young people and listen to them.

16. The leaders report regularly to the appropriate church councils.

17. The minister is supportive of the group and its leaders and visits regularly.

18. The group has at least one camp each year.

19. The group attends combined youth events at a regional level.

20. The leaders regularly introduce new and creative program ideas.

21. The group adopts a service or outreach project.

Are there any keys which you would wish to add to this list?

Place a tick (   ) against those factors which your church achieves well.

Place an arrow (   ) against those factors which your church needs to improve.

Again, this activity may be done individually or discussed by a group of leaders. If you like, make your own list of '21 keys to a slack group for young people'!

You might like to use WORKSHEET 22 to take an honest look at your groups.

How do we plan a good program?

After your group one night, three young people approach you as the leaders with a list of complaints. They are:
* the program is boring
* the group never does anything new
* no-one knows ahead of time what the program will be
* the leaders seem to be unprepared each week
* they would be embarrassed to bring their friends because of these things.

How would you as a leader reply?

....
....

....
....
....
....

Good planning is the key to effective programming. Kids know when time and effort has been put into a good program. They appreciate variety and new ideas. Both regular participants and potential group members benefit from a program printed in advance. A well organised program also reduces stress on the leadership team because each person knows ahead of time what needs to be done.

However, many groups don't take the time to plan well, and their youth ministry suffers.

Young people have unique characteristics and needs because of their ages and stages of development. It's important that group programs are aimed at meeting these needs. Mary-Ruth Marshall, in *It's Tuesday Night Again*, lists five areas of need.

1. IDENTITY – the need to develop a positive self-image and individual maturity.
2. INDEPENDENCE – the need to learn to make adult decisions and be responsible.

3. INTIMACY – the need to develop close, caring relationships with peers.
4. INSPIRATION – the need to develop hopes and ideals to direct their future.

5. INVESTMENT – the need to develop commitment to one's values and beliefs.

What are some ways in which group programs may meet these needs?

IDENTITY

INDEPENDENCE

INTIMACY

INSPIRATION

INVESTMENT

Psychologist A.H. Maslow developed a theory of the needs of people which he places in a hierarchy of importance.

Maslow's hierarchy of human needs

On the whole, a person cannot devote energy towards the satisfaction of needs at one level until the needs of the levels below are satisfied to a reasonable extent.

What are some of the implications of this for youth group programming?

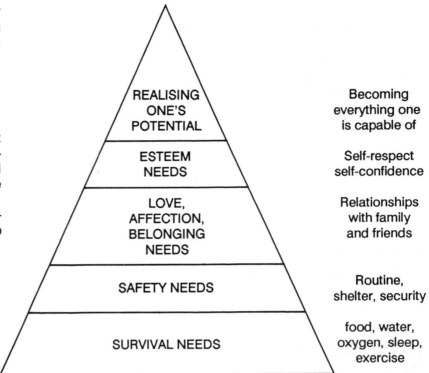

REALISING ONE'S POTENTIAL — Becoming everything one is capable of

ESTEEM NEEDS — Self-respect self-confidence

LOVE, AFFECTION, BELONGING NEEDS — Relationships with family and friends

SAFETY NEEDS — Routine, shelter, security

SURVIVAL NEEDS — food, water, oxygen, sleep, exercise

A basic planning process

Here is a simple approach to program planning which could be used on a three-monthly basis.

1. Who plans?

Think about who should attend the planning meeting.

There should be both leaders and young people, depending upon the age of the group members and the number of leaders per group.

By involving young people you help develop their leadership potential.

Arrange the planning meeting well beforehand to ensure good attendance.

Planning meeting

Date:...

Venue:...

....

Who will come

....

....

....

....

....

....

....

....

2. Who comes

Who are you planning for
Begin by reminding yourselves of the make-up of your group along with any potential newcomers.

Age group: ....

Average attendance: ....

Other information about their needs and interests:

....

....

....

....

....

....

3. Set aims and objectives

Develop some general aims for your program and some specific objectives which would help fulfil those aims.

For example,

AIMS

   To build a caring group

OBJECTIVES

   – Plan 'getting-to-know you' activities.

   – Visit each person's home for supper.

   – Do a simulation game on interdependence.

4. Gather ideas and resources

Brainstorm ideas related to meeting your objectives and aims. List every possible idea and try to be as creative as possible.

Use a variety of resources such as magazines, people, books for ideas.

5. Plan

Choose the best ideas from your list of possibilities. Think about what kinds of activities have worked well in the past.

Check presbytery and synod events so that your dates don't clash.

Write out your weekly plan of programs, keeping a balance between nights at home and away.

Use a planning sheet. See WORKSHEET 23, at the end of this chapter, for a sample planning sheet.

6. Check

That the plans meet the aims and objectives.

Any potential problems (wet weather) and contingency plans. Any long-term arrangements which need to be made (bookings of venues, speakers).

Identify anything which may require the approval of your minister or elders.

7. Responsibility

Major areas of responsibility should be identified as far ahead as possible.

Make sure you write down who is supposed to do what.

Do detailed planning of who does what 4-6 weeks ahead.

Check that these things have been organised.

   – Venue, unlocking and set up

   – transport

   – Picking up equipment to be borrowed

   – Advertising

   – Preparing devotions

   – Contacting guest speakers

8. Follow up

Assign one or two people to be in charge of the evening. They will be responsible for checking that others have done their jobs.

Map out a detailed plan of the evening. See WORKSHEET 24, at the end of this chapter, for a sample plan.

9. Setting up

Be ready before the kids arrive.

Make time to pray about the program beforehand.

Make sure the venue is set up properly with all equipment operating.

Make sure everyone understands what they have to do.

Set a good, friendly atmosphere.

Start on time.

Work to time, but be flexible if certain activities go very well or very badly.

Support each other in leadership.

Clean up afterwards.

10. Evaluation

Always evaluate activities in relation to your original aims and objectives.

Ask 'what worked well, and why?' and 'what could have been better, and how?'

Evaluate leaders' contributions to the activity – give constructive feedback.

Return all equipment and write thank you letter if appropriate.

Follow-up any issues and/or concerns arising from the activities.

General

* It is important that the young people themselves feel involved in the organising and running of the group. As a leader you must be sensitive to the abilities of the group and allow them to organise to the extent of their ability. This will vary for each group.

Some tips to running your meeting night

Before the meeting

a) Contact any invited guests (speakers or other groups) to confirm arrangements and to see that there are no last minute hitches.

Check that they have transport and know where and when to meet you. Confirm what you expect of them, and answer any questions they have.

Thank them for being prepared to come.

b) Check and confirm bookings of places or transport which you intend using.

c) Check that all leaders know and understand the parts of the program assigned to them.

d) Check all equipment which is to be used. Where this is to be borrowed or hired, do so in plenty of time to make alternative arrangements if necessary. With some equipment you will need to check that you are able to use it.

e) Undertake whatever publicity you consider helpful. Consult your delivery, mailing, telephone, visiting lists. Use notice boards and parish news sheets and other inexpensive media.

f) Ensure that participants are aware of anything they need to have done, or to bring, at the previous meeting of the group.

g) Insist on a punctual start to the meeting.

h) Pray.

At the meeting

1) Upon arrival at the meeting, the young people are keen to get moving straight away. They want activity with little or no explanation that will get things moving. After a warm up, members are more prepared to listen to explanations.

2 Present the program with confidence in yourself – the result of planning and experience. Have confidence in the group's ability and assure them that they have your confidence.

3) Enthusiastic leaders generally have an enthusiastic group, because enthusiasm is catching.

4) Generally follow the planned program and keep to the allocated time. This is the guarantee of meeting objectives.

5) Avoid prolonged pauses and do not have people sitting, singing or listening too long. The program needs to flow smoothly so that interest is maintained and periods of inactive boredom do not occur.

6) Never allow any activity to go on too long. Finish it when the group wants more, rather than when they have had too much and never want to see it again. Be quick to detect signs of fatigue or boredom and change the program to suit.

7) If a planned activity does not 'click' after a trial run, take it off and provide a substitute. Have sufficient spare activities available so the program can be changed to suit the mood of the group or the number present.

8) Maintain control of the group. Never shout. Never discipline a person in front of the group, but take the individual aside. In this way you will maintain that person's respect in the eyes of the group and increase respect for yourself. Use humour, but nor sarcasm. Call young people by name. Only make a threat if you intend to carry it out. Have only a few necessary rules, but see they are kept. If you use a whistle, do so sparingly and ensure that all know what it means. The whistle is rightly a piece of game equipment.

9) If you have some difficult young people, give them something to do; make friends with them; give the leader some responsibility; split them and involve them with others. If they refuse to co-operate, warn them privately and if necessary expel them from the group for a period of time.

10) Learn the difference between noise that comes from enjoyment and noise that comes from disorder. Tolerate the former to a comfortable level, but discourage the latter. Know the local regulations on the use of amplified noise at night.

11) Try to involve everybody at once if possible Avoid elimination games by changing them into an awarding of points. Never leave people standing around with nothing to do, unless everybody knows that this is a time set aside for talking. In this case, music provides a good background for private conversation.

Guidelines for running a game and similar activity

a) Know the activity thoroughly and ensure you have all the necessary equipment.
b) Have equipment ready and the area marked out, or else while you move to the next step, an assistant could do this.
c) Briefly explain the activity while the group is seated and quiet.
d) Give a demonstration or trial run where practical. Have a handful of individuals you have taught already, and let them demonstrate.
e) Ask for questions.
f) Commence the activity.
g) During the activity, new rules may be introduced – modify rules to suit the group.

Remember to:

1) Keep explanation of activity and rules to a minimum.
   • reduce initial explanation
   • speeds up the start of the game
   • ensures players only have a little to assimilate at any one time.

2) If you encourage team spirit on a competitive basis, take care it does not extend to the point where competition is taken so seriously that group spirit is lost.

'So you ...'

A leaders' awareness game for those who wish to anticipate and thus prevent disaster.

Rules

In small groups, in turn discuss what you personally would do in the following situations. The rest of the group comments on your answer, and affirms it, improves it or makes alternative suggestions.

Suggestions

1. You have prepared a three month program for your group, and the group has just informed you that it doesn't want your program. So you ...

2. You have a small group within your fellowship who don't join in, but sit and joke about those who do. So you ...

3. You have, in a consultative way, put together a program, but one carload of kids won't even come inside. Rather they prefer to talk outside and occasionally burn up and down the street. This creates divided loyalties for those inside. So you ...

4. Two or three dominant people in your group take over at every opportunity. Their attention seeking behaviour, and loudness is very disruptive. So you ...

5. Your kids only turn up to those nights they like (skating etc.) and on the other nights you are reduced to the faithful few. So you ...

6. Your group is divided into fun loving types and Bible study types. You wish to help the group grow closer together. So you ...

7. You wish to run a dance (as an outreach) program, but meet opposition from some of the church people. So you ...

8. You plan a camp for your thirty strong youth group and only nine decide to come. So you ...

9. You delegate parts of an evening program to group participants who turn up unprepared. So you ...

10. A group participant is leading a segment of program in a very inadequate way and the group is being inattentive. So you ...

11. You have planned a film night, but the projector won't work. So you ...

12. You have a 'you beaut' program, but no-one ever turns up on time for the start. So you ...

13. Your program is constantly interrupted by people in the group disappearing for a smoke, a drink, or to be alone with their boyfriend/girlfriend. So you ...

14. Your group tells you it will run its own program and you need not come. You doubt their ability. So you ...

Data collection checklist

The group participants

WHO are they – individually?
WHAT are they like – as a group?
WHAT have they been doing (last couple of years)?
— within the church
— outside the church?
WHAT is the age range?
SEXES?
WHAT schools are attended within the group?
WHAT is the social setting of the area?
WHAT do they see as successes?
— as failures?

WHAT is their relationship to the church?
WHAT is their relationship to their parents and friends?

WHAT other attractions (clubs, organisations) are there for them within the community?

The church

* What are the 'limits for structure'? Sunday nights only? Can we have special events? Special worship services? Trips/outings? Church-inns? Recreation? What meal arrangements are possible? Can we do a musical? A play?
* If your church has a regular fellowship meeting or family night meal, can the young people be responsible for a program? Can the young people and congregation have joint activities?
* What facilities are available for worship services, recreation etc.?
* Does your church approve of meeting as the other youth group etc.?

Use WORKSHEETS 25 and 26 at the end of this chapter to help you identify your program aims and objectives and relate these to specific events you are planning.

Resources

People	— what people are available to lead
	— what talents do leaders have
	— what talents do parents have
	— what talents do members of the church have
	— what other people are available
Places	— what places are there available to meet within the church (church hall, stage, vestries, kitchen, porch, grounds),
	— is there lighting for night (tower etc.)
	— are there places available within walking distance (pools, parks, vacant allotments, empty warehouses etc.)
Equipment	— what is available (projectors, screens, cameras, tape recordings, record players, cassettes, O.H.P., duplicating facilities etc.)
	— how do you obtain equipment
	— what equipment needs to be purchased
	— what can be borrowed from people, schools, Teacher Resource Centres, other churches etc – use initiative in use of existing equipment
	— what can be made by the group
Event	— Check presbytery and synod events before you plan your calendar
	— check school, community and church calendar to see which activities can be incorporated and which organised around
	— find out what other groups are doing and whether it is possible to combine
	— check leadership training days to allow leaders to be free
Finance	— what money is available
Information	— what books are available, need to be purchased
	— put group leaders names on mailing lists
	— find out about present youth culture
	— record past programs
	— subscribe to magazines e.g. *A.D.*
	— look for leaders etc.

How do we know what programs young people will like?

Michelle went to a drama workshop at a youth leaders' training day and learnt some great ideas for doing role plays with her youth group. At Youth Group the following Friday she thought she'd get the kids to improvise a situation as part of devotions. When she asked for volunteers, no one put up their hand. She picked a couple of kids, who both giggled so much that devotions were a disaster. Michelle vowed she'd never try a role play again.

Every group is different, and what works in one place may not work in another. Different age groups tend to enjoy different kinds of activities.

Some basic guidelines to follow are:

* the younger the group, the more active the program
* the younger the group, the shorter is their attention span
* the older the group, the more easily they will discuss issues
* the older the group, the more easily they will get involved in creative activities
* the older the group, the more choices they will want concerning what to do and how to do it
* the older the group, the more interested they are in activities with the opposite sex
* the younger the group, the more they prefer competitive activities.

Surveys by the Joint Board of Christian Education of Church Youth Groups reveal preferences for activities. (See Chapter 1 pages 11-13.)

The easiest way to find out what programs your young people like is to ask them. Use WORKSHEET 27 as an interest-finder before you plan your next program.

What are some good program ideas?

Where do we begin? Firstly, the best program ideas are not the ones that worked last year. Variety is the key to successful programming. If you're still doing the duster hockey, chalk chases and progressive dinners, chances are that your kids are getting bored. While it may be easy on you as a leader to repeat the same old ideas, your group will be much more appreciative of a program with plenty of surprises.

1. Seek out good resources

The first thing to know is that there are plenty of books and magazines with great program ideas such as:

50 Fun Programs That Work With Youth Geraldine Anderson, ed., JBCE

What Will We Do On Friday Night? Glen Smyth, JBCE

Group Magazine's *Best Youth Group Programs*, Group Books

Group Magazine's *Best Junior High Meetings*, Group Books

A.D. magazine with Leader's Guide, JBCE

2. Swap good ideas

Meet with other youth leaders and swap ideas with them every few months. Regional youth councils are a good place to do this.

3. Use local people and places

A good starting point is your local church and community. Often good ideas are right under your nose; interesting places and people are nearby and available.

Here's a list of possible 'place' resources:

Airport
Ambulance Station
Amusement Park/Parlour
Aquarium
Arcade
Archery Field
Art Gallery
Bakery
Bank Vault
Basketball Court
Beach
Blacksmith
Boat Wharf
Botanic Gardens
Bowling Alley
Canoe club

Car Racing Circuit
Caves
Cemetery
Church
Clinic
Coffee Shop
Crematorium
Dam
Defence establishment
Discotheque
Docks
Drive-in
Exhibition
Factory
Farm
Ferry
Fire Station
Fishing Spot
Football Field
Gaol
Garbage Dump
Gasworks
Golf Course
Hospital
Infirmary
Judo Club
Kennels
Kilns

Laboratory
Lake
Law Court
Lighthouse
Lookout
Minister's Manse
Motor Show
Museum
Naval Base
Oil Refinery
Orchard
Orphanage
Picture Theatre
Pig Farm
Police Station
Quarry
Radio Station
Railway Station
Reservoir
Rest Home
Restaurant
Rocks
School
Shrine
Skating Rink
Snow Field
Squash Court
Swimming Pool

Synagogue
Telephone Exchange
Television Studio
Train
University
Veterinary Surgery
Warehouse
Waterworks
Waxworks
X-ray Laboratory
Yacht Club
Yoga Club
Zoo

If you seriously want to consider all possibilities, then first compile a list from a telephone book – yellow pages, too.

Hopefully these ideas will get you thinking about ways of updating your own programs.

5. Be creative

Don't simply rely on using other people's ideas. Try to invent your own. The main thing is that you need to allow yourself and others the time and space to do this.

How will people know what's happening with the group?

'I wonder what's on at youth group tonight?' Chris and Sue were talking on their way to the church. 'I hope its not another games night', said Sue. Chris nodded agreement. As they turned the corner, they saw people piling into cars. 'Hurry up you two', shouted Tony, their leader, 'We're going skating tonight'! 'I haven't got any socks with me!' said Chris, who was wearing thongs. 'I wish I'd

known', said Sue. 'Ruth would have loved to come'. 'Well I'm sorry', replied Tony, 'we only decided yesterday. We couldn't exactly ring everybody'. So off they went.

Publicity, or the lack of it, can sometimes make or break a good program. Some groups seem to operate on the principle that you can find out what's happening when you arrive. This can cause

a whole range of unnecessary and unhelpful problems:
* parents don't know exactly what their kids are doing
* the leaders seem disorganised (often true)
* the group participants are indifferent towards a program they know nothing about
* few new people attend because of lack of information to attract them

* ministers and elders may have lack of confidence in the leaders, or at least lack of knowledge of what goes on.

In contrast to this, a well-publicised program can contribute positively to the growth and atmosphere of the group.

* it advises parents exactly what is happening and when
* leaders themselves know what is going on from week to week
* young people know what to expect before they arrive, especially if they need to bring something or meet at a special time
* special events may be anticipated and attract extra people (boring events probably shouldn't be on the program in the first place)
* parents of newcomers have a point of contact with the group

* the minister and elders are well-informed of what is happening.

Tips for good publicity

1. Produce a printed program on a term basis.

2. Print coming activities in the church newsletter a week ahead (longer for special events).

3. Get the term program photocopied or off-set printed on coloured paper for best results.

4. If you have access to a computer, use graphics, otherwise rub-on lettering.

5. Add pictures, either your own drawings or buy one of the many clip-art books available.

6. Make the program interesting by designing it as something unusual e.g. a record cover, a menu, a crossword, a movie guide.

7. Be sure to include the following details:
   * meeting date
   * regular venue and any changes
   * leaders' names and phone numbers
   * cost of any programs
   * starting and finishing times (along with any exceptions)
   * the name of the church to which the group belongs
   * whether help with transport is required

8. Distribute the program at least 3 weeks ahead of its starting date.

9. Have a contingency plan for phoning young people in the event of last-minute changes

10. See if you can distribute the programs through the local schools.

How do we improve our group?

Once there was a little fish who was looking for the ocean. It asked an older fish which said, 'Why, you're swimming in it'. The little fish replied, 'Don't be silly, this is just water' – and went on looking.

Often the answers to our questions are right under our noses but we still don't see them. Youth leaders may at times feel frustrated by the lack of growth, direction or numbers in their youth group. The main reason that changes and improvements don't occur is that we may fail to carefully identify the problems and work towards adequate solutions.

How do we evaluate our programs?

Evaluation is a key phase of any ministry or event. There are several simple steps in any evaluation process.

1. Gather feedback from participants and leaders – what worked well and what didn't. Did the program meet aims and expectations?

2. Identify positive and negative factors
Why did some things work well?
Why did other things not go well?

3. Identify positive alternatives
Describe problem areas in more detail.
How are people feeling?
What people, events or environment caused this?
Describe how you hope things could be different next time.
Brainstorm factors which could help such an improvement.
Identify factors which could hinder such an improvement.

4. Choose positive actions
Choose a couple of positive, achievable actions from your brainstorming list.
Identify people and resources necessary to accomplish these steps.
Set a time line for beginning and ending this action.
Give positive feedback to people responsible for positive factors in 2 above.

5. Follow through positive actions
Carry out actions identified in step 4.

6. EVALUATE
Begin again at step 1.

Note that:
Evaluation should be an ongoing process, not an annual event.
Evaluation should involve all parties concerned at various times – leaders, group members, ministers, parents, elders.
Evaluation should be constructive, not destructive, because it aims to make ministry more effective. (This doesn't mean that evaluation won't result in stopping some activities or groups).

The basic questions in evaluation relate to:

1. People's experience of the event – not just what they think but also how they feel.

2. Preparation – was it adequate and appropriate?

3. Objectives – In what ways were the objectives met or not met?

4. Activities – Which methods and activities were helpful or effective?
– Which were ineffective?
– How could these activities be improved next time?

5. Leadership – What leader's roles and actions were helpful and appropriate? Which were inappropriate?

6. Participation – What actions/responses were appropriate or inappropriate? What reasons can be identified for these?

7. Organisation – How appropriate was the organisational structure? In what ways could it be adapted or improved for greater effectiveness?

8. Group Life – How has the quality of the group's life been enhanced? (Don't just evaluate activities.)

9. Follow-on – How will the results of the evaluation be processed?

Use WORKSHEETS 28 and 29 with your group or leaders to help evaluate your programs.

WORKSHEET 21: Possible purposes for friendship and fun groups

Here are some possible purposes for a fun and friendship group. Rank them in what you see as their priority in your church (1 = first, 2 = second etc.)

Actual Priority	Ideal Priority	
		To help youth understand the Christian faith.
		To help youth respect and be friendly to others.
		To help youth become a part of the church.
		To help youth accept Jesus as Saviour and Lord.
		To help youth with personal problems.
		To help youth understand the Bible.
		To help youth learn right from wrong.
		To provide a place for young people to be with friends.
		To help youth understand themselves.
		To give young people the chance to help others.
		To help young people accept responsibility.
		To help young people become friends.
		To give non-church youth a point of contact with the church.

(This list is adapted from *12-14 Year Olds in the Church* by Mary-Ruth Marshall, JBCE.)

WORKSHEET 22: An honest look at our group

1. Does this group have a fixed purpose? ....

2. If so, what is that purpose? ....

....

3. Is the purpose being achieved?

....

4. If you think the group has no purpose or the wrong purpose, what kind of purpose do you think it should have?

....

....

5. What do you appreciate most about the group?

....

6. What do you appreciate least about the group?

....

7. Should any changes be made? If so, what are they? ....

....

8. Has this group helped you or others to grow in Christian faith? If so, how?

....

....

9. Do your aims as a member (or interested person) agree with the aims of the group?

....

10. Is there anything distinctive about this group which appeals to you? (something other groups don't have)

....

....

11. Have you learnt anything important through this group?

....

....

WORKSHEET 23: Sample quarterly program

		WHAT'S ON	ORGANISER	WORSHIP	OTHER EVENTS
February	9	Welcome back Whoopee night	John and Claire	Jan	
	16	Sound Scavenger Hunt	Mike	Gail	
	23	Old Time Dance	Ron and Marian	Andrew	
March	2	Discussion on Unemployment	Fred	Bill	*Don't forget* Youth Rally on Saturday 3rd. Meet at Church 6.45 p.m.
	9	Nite Hike (and Camp fire)	Jan	Mike	
	16	Simulation Game on Poverty	John	Claire	*Don't forget* Youth Club leads worship on 25th March. Andrew and Marian need help with this service.
	23	Kite Making	Bill	Fred	Kite Flying (hopefully) 24th March
	30	Indoor Games Night	Anne	Rev. Bloggs	
April	6	Progressive Supper	Ron	Marian	
	13	EASTER YOUTH CAMP (12th – 16th) at Blogg's Bay (Register with Bill by March 23rd)			
	20	Fete Preparation Night	Gail	Mike	
	27	Car Rally	Gail	Rodney	

WORKSHEET 24: Sample evening program

Evening Program for   / /

THEME – SOUND SCAVENGER HUNT
ORGANISER – MIKE

WHAT	WHY	WHEN		WHO	WHERE	HOW	EVALUATION
1. Arrive and settle down	Create fellowship	15 min	7.30	Jill	Main Hall	General mixing – singing if requested	
2. Explanation of Sound Hunt	Avoid confusion	6 min	7.45	Mike	Main Hall	Sitting in a close group	
3. Break in groups	Necessary for task	4 min	7.51	Mike	Main Hall	Each corner of hall	
4. Hand out equipment	Necessary for task	5 min	7.55	Jill	Main Hall	One volunteer each group	
5. Hand out list of items at 2 min intervals	Necessary for task	2 min intervals	8.00 8.02 8.04 8.06 8.08	Mike	Main Hall	One volunteer each group	
6. All return and settle down	Necessary for task		9.00	to Mike	Main Hall	In groups	
7. Play back findings	Enjoyment	20 min	9.05	Each group	Main Hall	According to plan	
8. Sing	Lead to devotions	6 min	9.25	Jill	Around stage	Sit on floor	
9. Devotions	To help kids grow at depth	10 min	9.31	Gail (theme is listening)	Around stage	Sit on floor	
10. Supper	The peasants are hungry	15 min	9.41	John	In kitchen	With usual chaos	
11. Clean up and end	To get home	—	10.00	Mike	—	—	

WORKSHEET 25: Identifying program aims and objectives

		Rating as at present	Rating as should be	Possible Objectives
Identity Aims	To help kids clarify who they are			
Relationship and Group Building Aims	To help kids relate to each other in positive ways; as well as to the wider world of home, school and society			
Decision Making Aims	To help kids grow in their ability to make wise decisions in relation to their personal lives, finance, jobs, and members of their opposite sex			
Organisational Aims	To keep the group going and get more members			
Church Related Aims	To have young people become confirmed (or full) members of the church			
Faith Aims	To bring young people into a living relationship with Jesus Christ as Saviour and Lord			
Fun Aims	To provide a secure environment where kids can let down their hair and enjoy themselves			
Counselling Aims	To provide a place where kids can come and find people who will listen carefully to them, and care deeply about them, their joys and their hurts			
Skill Aims	To provide opportunities to learn new skills and to develop latent creative and leadership abilities			
Theological	To enable kids to explore and examine the Christian faith so that they will come to a deeper understanding of what it is all about			
Lifestyle Aims	To model the Christian lifestyle in such a way that kids will see it as an attractive and viable alternative to the other styles of life they see around them.			

How to work with young people. Copyright © 1991 The Joint Board of Christian Education

WORKSHEET 26: Event planner

EVENT/SESSION:..

DATE/TIME:...

PEOPLE RESPONSIBLE:...

....

....

AIM: (General statement of what you want to achieve)

....

....

OBJECTIVES: (Specific statement of what you want to achieve)

....

....

TIME	WHAT IS GOING TO HAPPEN (i.e. **HOW** you will achieve your objectives)	WHO	EQUIPMENT

WORKSHEET 27: Interest finder

Tick **all** the activities that interest you.

Aboriginal culture night
Abseiling
Aeroplane modelling
Animals
April Fools night
Archery
Art
Astronomy
Baby night
Badminton
Banner making
Barbecue
Basketball
Beach trip
Bike riding
Board games
Boating
Boomerang throwing
Bowling
Bush dancing
Bushwalking
Camping
Candle making
Canoeing
Car rally
Car wash
Cards
Career night
Caving
Charades
Clay modelling
Concert
Cooking
Craft
Creative movement
Culture night
Dancing
Debates
Drama
Earth ball game

Embroidery
Fabric painting
Fashion parade
First aid
Fishing
Football
Frisbee games
Grass skiing
Guest speakers
Gymnastics
Hay ride
Hike
Hiroshima Day
Horse riding
Ice skating
Jewellery making
Kite flying
Lamington drive
Leather craft
Lino block printing
Lock-in
Macrame
Mini-bikes
Mini-Olympics
Mock wedding
Modelling
Movies
Music
Mystery hike
Netball
New games
Newspaper visit
Origami
Orienteering
Painting
Paper making
Paper planes
Patchwork
Photography
Picnics

Pizza making
Pottery
Puppets
Putt-putt
Puzzles
Quizzes
Raft-building
Record/tape night
Rock climbing
Roller skating
Sailing
Scavenger hunt
Self defence
Silk-screen painting
Simulation games
Singing
Skateboarding
Skiing
Slot car racing
Softball
Square dancing
Squash
Surf skiing
Surfing
Swimming
Table tennis
Tennis
Train ride
Treasure hunt
Video making
Volleyball
Walkathon
Weaving
Windsurfing
Working bee
Yachting
Yo-yo's
Zoo visit

Name ....

WORKSHEET 28: Evaluating our youth programs

	USUALLY	SOMETIMES	RARELY
1. Do you get going punctually with an activity that gets the group moving and requires little organisation?			
2. Are you confident in yourself and in your members? (This comes through planning and experience.)			
3. Are you enthusiastic?			
4. Do you generally keep to the program and allocated times?			
5. Do you avoid prolonged pauses and ensure the program flows smoothly?			
6. Do you finish an activity when the group wants more or does it go on too long?			
7. Can you maintain control of the group never shout use humour call members by name?			
8. Do you plan to involve everyone?			
9. Do you have a change of face up front?			
10. Do you know well what you are doing and what is happening next?			

What do you need to improve on in your presentation?

....

....

....

....

WORKSHEET 29: An evaluation process

STEP 1.   DESCRIBE THE PROBLEM:

....

....

....

....

STEP 2.   ANALYSE PROBLEM AREAS

A. WHO ARE THE PEOPLE INVOLVED?

....

....

....

....

B. WHAT ARE THESE PEOPLE EXPERIENCING AND FEELING?

....

....

....

....

C. WHAT EVENTS HAVE CONTRIBUTED TO THIS SITUATION?

....

....

....

....

D. WHAT OTHER FACTORS ARE IMPORTANT?

....

....

....

....

STEP 3.   IDENTIFY POSITIVE ALTERNATIVES

A.   DESCRIBE YOUR HOPE FOR THE SITUATION IN POSITIVE TERMS

....

....

....

....

B.   LIST POSITIVE FACTORS WHICH COULD CONTRIBUTE TO THIS CHANGE

....

....

....

....

C.   IDENTIFY FACTORS WHICH COULD HINDER THIS IMPROVEMENT

....

....

....

....

STEP 4.   CHOOSE POSITIVE ACTIONS

A.   CHOOSE A COUPLE OF POSITIVE ACTIONS FROM 3B

....

....

....

....

B.   IDENTIFY THE PEOPLE AND RESOURCES NECESSARY TO ACCOMPLISH THESE

ACTION NO.	PEOPLE	RESOURCES	OTHER

C. SET A TIME FOR THESE ACTIONS

ACTION NO.   START BY   FINISH BY

....

....

....

....

....

....

STEP 5.   IDENTIFY A MEANS OF FURTHER EVALUATION

DATE: ....

PLACE: ....

PEOPLE: ....

PROCESS: ....

....

....

....

....

....

Chapter 8

Discipleship groups

Discipleship groups

Where does discipleship fit into youth ministry?   115

What role will your group play in discipleship?   115

The value of small groups   116

The role of the Bible in growing disciples   117

Going deeper in groups   119

How will young people develop their spirituality?   120

WORKSHEET 30: Sample plan for a discipleship group   121

WORKSHEET 31: Study suggestions   122

Where does discipleship fit into youth ministry?

A disciple = a learner.
A Christian disciple = a learner of Christ.

How do we assist young people who have come to the point of discipleship to own the faith and live their lives as Christians? Discipleship is about deepening faith and its connections with everyday life.

The Uniting Church in Australia *Young People and Your Church Action Manual* states the biggest challenge to the church is to take seriously the need to provide young people with some discipleship training.

Understanding what it means to be Christian today requires more than an effort to do the right thing. Discipleship involves a deeper understanding of the gospel and its implications for our lives and responding to God through putting self last and God first. This understanding and commitment doesn't stem from an occasional prayer or song at a friendship and fun group but through young people questioning, discussing and studying the Bible, relating it to their lives.

Why we need a friendship and fun group and a discipleship group

With this in mind we need to recognise that not all young people are at the point where they are ready to take seriously the challenge of being a disciple. Some are just looking for a setting where they can meet people, feel accepted for who they are and enjoy themselves.

Attempting to meet both needs in one group usually results with neither task being done properly and young people feeling their needs are not being met.

Those who run youth programs know how difficult it is to provide solid training for young Christians in a group in which most young people do not profess a faith or do not accept the authority of the Bible.

To make real discipleship training effective, a group is needed in which people share some common starting point of faith. It is essential for churches to put new effort into nurturing young Christians – equipping them with solid biblical teaching and the exploration of the meaning for all the aspects of life with a living relationship with Jesus Christ.

Young People and Your Church Action Manual. Uniting Church Press, 1989, page 13.

What role will your group play in discipleship?

To provide the most effective program a church ideally needs to provide two different groups:

1. A friendship and fun group which has an emphasis on young people getting together for enjoyable activities as part of the church's programs.

2. A discipleship group which has an emphasis on opportunities to explore and discuss issues about faith.

Both these groups should be open to young people who understand the nature of the groups and accept their emphasis and type of program. It will frequently be the case that the friendship and fun group will be larger than the discipleship group.

What is a discipleship group like?

It's a group that explores faith commitment and works towards developing a more mature faith and more active discipleship. It will allow young people to:
– meet as Christians who want to explore their faith
– study the Bible
– be taught what it means to be a disciple of Jesus Christ in today's world
– explore the connections between Christian faith and practical expression of what faith means for how they live in their community and the world
– explore their doubts and beliefs and pray together
– put what is learnt into practice
– find out more about faith even if they are a non-Christian.

These groups, would be held at a time suitable to the participants, an evening, a Sunday morning or afternoon, over a meal even breakfast. The group should plan its life and make it a priority. It is not necessary to have a group that meets every week. Even once a month would make it possible to provide special encouragement to deeper faith.

What will be the guidelines of this group?

Sometimes it will be important for the group to decide on a common purpose and agree on basic guidelines that will build and mould the life of the group.

For that kind of group there may sometimes be a statement of expectations such as the following:

1. **Attendance** – priority is given to the group meetings.
Except in cases of emergency, you will be present and on time.

2. **Participation** – part of the purpose of the group is to get acquainted and build a sense of oneness or 'koinonia'. This is accomplished by letting each person in the group tell his or her spiritual story. To be a participant, you must be willing to let the group hear your story.

3. **Confidentiality** – anything that is shared in the group is kept in strict confidence. This is not a therapy group, but information will be shared from time to time that should not be repeated outside the group.

4. **Accountability** – at the close of every session, an opportunity may be given for you to share new goals you want to set for your life. When you state a goal and ask the others in the group to support you in these goals, you are giving permission to the group to hold you accountable.

5. **Accessibility** – the group is for people who know they need the help of others to overcome temptation, spiritual depression, and weakness. In deciding to be in a group, you are admitting you need support and that you are willing to support others in the same condition.

The value of small groups

Small groups can contribute a great deal to young people in their development as disciples of Christ.

John Mallison who is experienced with small groups and has written much about them in Australia says the values are:

A. For the individual

1. Growing awareness of the presence of God's Spirit at work in his/her life.
2. The increasing ability to get in touch with feelings, that is, a growing self awareness.
3. Healing in areas of life where deep emotional hurts exist.
4. Have a sense of belonging and security.

5. Growing sense of self worth.
6. Become aware of and have opportunity to exercise spiritual gifts.
7. Come to an understanding of how one affects others in the group and hence improve skills in relating.
8. Experience real Christian fellowship and personal spiritual renewal.
9. Become a more effective channel for God's love to others.

B. For the group

1. Become a caring, supportive, challenging community.
2. Work together towards a common goal.
3. Share a sense of commitment.

4. Experience real Christian fellowship.

5. Learn small group processes.

6. Experience praise and worship.

7. Communicate feelings and ideas openly and honestly.

C. For the local church

1. Bring about renewal.

2. Help the church to function as a body using the spiritual gifts of all its members.

3. Allow for proper ventilation of feelings in a supportive atmosphere and reduce the risk of division.

4. Overcome the inadequacies of present church structure which prevent people from coming into deep personal relationships.

5. Provide what secular society does not provide, in-depth personal encounter.

6. Increase awareness of God working in the lives of church people.

7. Grow in concern for people outside the church.

8. Provide a fellowship for new converts to the faith to be disciples and to grow.

9. Help bring a church to spiritual maturity.

10. Experience true church fellowship.

11. Add to the praise and worship of the body.

12. Make faith a living thing.

D. For the universal church

1. Bring spiritual vitality.

2. Help break down denominational barriers as people from various denominations experience unity of the Spirit.

3. Provide stimulus for growth and outreach.

E. For the world

1. Help to make the church a place where non Christians can experience the love of God and sense the excitement.

2. Affect society by making Christians more aware and more active in social action.

3. Have the gospel presented to them by a church convicted of the message of the gospel.

The role of the Bible in growing disciples

Many Christian young people look on the Bible as important, even vital but somehow not as meaningful to them as it should be. They read it periodically. They take stabs at having personal devotions. But still the Scriptures don't come across to them as vital, exciting and life changing. They accept the Bible as God's word but they haven't yet experienced it as God's personal word to them. The youth leader thus has a great opportunity – the chance to help young people discover that the Bible is exciting and relevant to them, the chance to launch them on a life-long and ever-deepening study of Scripture.

To some young people, the Bible seems to speak in a very negative tone of voice.
God speaks in love.
God speaks with competence.
God's words can be experienced.

A leader can help young people discover what the Bible really says. The particular kinds of help you need to give them involve making sure that there is a specific goal for the study; that you know what to look for; that they have a method for the Bible search that will ensure they are successful. Finally, a leader can help organise the results so that what has been learned can be seen to be meaningful.

It is vital that young people understand what the Bible teaches. Growth as Christians is intimately connected with knowing God's revealed will. But the leaders' task extends beyond communicating biblical information. The real goal of Bible learning, is to lead learners beyond a grasp of information – to faith response and obedience to what God's word reveals.

Study methods

Four basic considerations for choosing methods.

1) Methods are to be chosen for their appropriateness to purpose, content, ages, characteristics of the group, and time available.

2) Use of a variety of methods can help a leader maintain interest.
   For example:

buzz groups
brainstorming
forum of experts
debate
research and reports
role playing
case study
lecture

3) When methods are conceived as a way to help in opening channels of communications between individuals, freeing them to contribute and to benefit from contributions of others, they become something more than 'techniques to secure participation'.

4) The physical arrangement of the room has much to do with effectiveness of the methods.

Different approaches to Bible study

a) Get an overview of the Bible as a whole – generally Bible study has been too piecemeal.

b) Work through one book of the Bible at a time.
c) Follow a subject or a theme.
d) Word study using key words e.g. covenant, Spirit.
e) Topical study – peace, prayer, call.
f) Devotional study – read a passage and reflect.
g) Relational – what does the story say to my story.

John Mallison's *Growing Christians in Small Groups* and Roberta Hestenes' *Using the Bible in Small Groups* provide in depth practical information on styles of using the Bible for study.

Serendipity Bible for small groups approach

Lyman Coleman and friends have produced Bible studies with the *New International Version* text on all passages of the Scripture using three sets of questions for each passage enabling par-

ticipants to dig deep into the Word and apply it to their lives.

The three sets of questions are:

OPEN: To break the ice in a group by allowing participants to share a page out of their own story – something funny, significant, or childhood related – and to prepare the group for Bible study.

DIG: For digging into the Scripture story to find out what's going on, what's the main idea, the plot, the argument, the spiritual principle, etc.

REFLECT: To apply the Scripture story to real life.

These questions allow individuals to take a personal inventory, and to share how they're going to apply the passage to their lives. And for advanced groups each book offers one or two comprehensive study tracks for exploring the book as a whole.

Going deeper in groups

A discipleship group is a particular kind of group. It is established specifically for the purpose of helping young people with faith to grow as disciples – to deepen their faith and to connect their faith with everyday living.

However many different kinds of groups can go deeper in their relationships between members and their exploration of faith.

Some groups may be interested to try the thirty day experiment.

The 30 day experiment – from the Pittsburg experiment

The Great Experiment puts together five spiritual disciplines: prayer, service, tithing, Bible study and Christian concern for others.

1. Meet once each week to pray together

This is a time of prayer, sharing and study, each given about half an hour. It includes silent as well as voluntary, spoken prayer; sharing of questions and problems as well as discoveries and experiences; study of helpful

books as well as the Bible. Groups are encouraged to keep records of prayer needs and results.

2. Give two hours time each week to God

Self-surrender is involved in such service. Here is a beginning list.

a) Visit hospital patients or shut-ins.
b) Visit members of the church to tell them about your experiences.
c) Visit families interested in the church and try to involve them.
d) Be a teacher or helper in a

Sunday school class for a month.

e) Join the choir for a month.

f) Visit your neighbourhood for one or two hours to visit potential church goers.

g) Spend an hour visiting two or three church families you do not know.

h) Visit new members of the church to get acquainted.

i) Help provide needed improvements, such as furnishings, shelving, curtains.

j) Be a telephone committee of one contacting people for the church.

k) Promote and maintain a church library during the month.

l) Work in your church office for one or two hours.

m) Work on the grounds of the church property – a continuing need.

n) Visit the homes of visitors to the church.

o) Use your imagination to discover other things the church needs you to do.

3. Give God 1/10 earnings during this month

Self-denial is part of tithing. Each person is encouraged to take the tithing out first and pray about how to effectively spend the other 9/10 of income.

4. Spend a half hour each day in prayer and meditation

Self-control is needed for this discipline! Here is the schedule:

10 minutes – Read Scripture for the day (see list below). Pray and meditate on this Scripture. Write out in less than 50 words how this passage applies to your life.

10 minutes. – Write out one totally unselfish and unexpected act of kindness or generosity that you will do today. Name the person – then act during the day, vigorously and with compassion and love. Keep a written record of the reaction of the person toward whom the kindness is extended, and the effect of this act upon you personally.

10 minutes. – Write out carefully how you would like to build and develop your life. Go into great detail if you desire. Take your time – be thoughtful and prayerful. One well prayed-out and thought-out sentence per day would be excellent progress.

Daily scriptures

1) 2 Chronicles 7:14
2) James 5:1
3) 1 John 3:22
4) John 15:6,7
5) Mark 11:24
6) Philippians 4:6
7) 1 John 5:14
8) Jeremiah 29:13
9) Matthew 6:7-13
10) Matthew 18:19
11) Isaiah 65:23,24
12) Matthew 6:6
13) Luke 11:9,10
14) Isaiah 58:9-11
15) Psalm 127:1
16) Psalm 66:18
17) Isaiah 59:1-3
18) Proverbs 28:9,10
19) Matthew 8:24
20) John 6:47
21) Ecclesiastes 3:1-8
22) Psalm 55:22
23) John 14:27
24) Psalm 1:1-3
25) John 14:1
26) Matthew 6:25-33
27) Psalms 23:1-6
28) Mark 12:30
29) Hebrews 12:1
30) John 4:14
31) Matthew 5:13-16.

5. Witness for God your experience to others

This natural expression may happen in the prayer group, with friends, on the telephone, or in the normal life of the church.

How will young people develop their spirituality?

How can we help them reflect on their faith and continue on their journey?

The answers to this question are many and appear in different forms throughout this book.

There are three areas which we would emphasise here.

1. The spiritual disciplines

Leaders may incorporate in study programs aspects of spiritual disciplines as mentioned by Richard Foster, in *Celebration of Discipline*:

the inward disciplines
  meditation
  prayer
  fasting
  study
the outward disciplines
  simplicity
  solitude
  submission
  service
the corporate disciplines
  confession
  worship
  guidance
  celebration.

2. The role of the church

Young people will grow in their faith as they take their place within the life of the church through worship, decision making, care and support, involvement in the community, through outreach and evangelism.

3. Role models

The friendship, the caring, the modelling that is offered to young people by leaders, ministers, elders, church members must never be under estimated.

The role of group leaders and their relationships with people in the group through friendship, caring, prayer will be essential.

It may be appropriate for some young people to have a spiritual director. This relationship would need to be at a level that is appropriate for the young person but include the opportunity to meet with a brother or sister in Christ once a month to check out spiritual development, attitudes to prayer and Bible reading and the other factors that are part of a young Christian growing in the faith.

WORKSHEET 30: Sample plan for a discipleship group

	What	How	Materials needed	Time allowed
1.	Arrive and settle down	Singing Listen to music		5 Mins
2.	Sharing time & Prayer	Share about life life since last met. Open prayer, someone to lead.		10 mins
3.	Introduction to theme/topic Reminder what (discussed last session)	Music Visuals Role Play		5 mins
4.	Presentation of theme/topic	See Video Set out drama Read or have read information Guest speaker Audio tape		10 mins
5.	Discussion of topic	Debate Questions Taking on role of character		15 mins
6.	Response	Fill out journal Identify strategy for action Write prayer, creed		10 mins
7.	Conclusion	Singing Prayers Benediction		5 mins

WORKSHEET 31: Study suggestions

Use these suggestions to guide your planning for a discipleship group.

A.D. magazine topics
Alcohol
Apostles' Creed
Baptism and the Lord's Supper
Beatitudes
Bible quiz
Bible study at camp
Bible study at coffee house
Biblical simulations
Building a Christian community
Capital punishment
Caravan trip
Career exploration
Censorship (TV, magazines, etc.)
Christian lifestyle at school
Christian living
Commitment
Communication workshop
Community concerns
Counselling centre testing
Criminal justice
Dating
Death
Death and dying (grief process)
Denominational beliefs
Denominational heritage
Discussion of sermons
Drugs
Environmental concerns
Eternal life and other options
Evangelism
Field trips
Forgiveness
Friendship
Galations
Global concerns
Handling conflict
Hunger
Identity

Intergenerational studies
 — on honesty
 — communication
 — values
 — biblical teachings
Jobs as Christian vocations
Joint Board of Christian Education curriculum topics
Lenten studies
 — Ash Wednesday Passion
 — Good Friday
 — Palm Sunday
 — Easter
Life and teachings of Jesus
Lifestyle
 — simplicity
 — conservation
Living the faith
Love
Making decisions
Mark
Marriage
Meaning of Jesus Christ
Moses
Movies
Music
 — modern
 — church
 — hymns
 — Christmas carols
Other denominations
Other religions
Overview of the Bible
Parables
Parent/youth relations
Passover and Holy Week
Paul
People of the Covenant – Old Testament
People who encountered Jesus

Poverty
Prayer and meditation
Prejudice/racism
Prepare mini-course for children
Prophecy
Prophets
Puppetry Workshop
Relationships
Revelation
Romans
School
Science fiction
Seasons of the church year denominational creeds
Sex/sexuality
Social issues
Spirituality/Confirmation/ commissioning
Stewardship
Students' rights
Study related to lectionary
Success
Symbols
The arts
The occult
The Ten Commandments
Twenty-third Psalm
Value process
Values clarification
Violence
visual arts
Weekly Bible study
What is a Christian?
Who is God?
Why poverty?
Women of the Bible
Women's movement
Worship
Youth issues

Chapter 9

Worship and devotions

Worship and devotions

How do we help young people understand what church worship is all about? — 125

How do we get young people involved in leading church worship? — 126

What are some creative worship ideas? — 127

Why should we have youth group devotions? — 129

How do we plan devotions which are creative, relevant and challenging? — 129

How do we make good use of music? — 131

WORKSHEET 32: How do you define worship? — 133

WORKSHEET 33: How meaningful is worship for me? — 134

WORKSHEET 34: Principles for planning worship — 135

WORKSHEET 35: Planning worship – order of service — 136

WORKSHEET 36: Worship planner — 137

WORKSHEET 37: A simple approach to planning devotions — 138

WORKSHEET 38: Reflection time at camp — 139

How do we help young people understand what church worship is all about?

'Church is boring' is a typical comment from teenagers. While many young people appreciate the opportunity to worship with a congregation, they also may find the music dull, the language over their heads, and the message irrelevant. Is this true for your congregation?

In response to this,

* we need to educate young people to understand what worship is
* we need to help them find meaningful ways of participating in worship
* we need to encourage people planning worship to make sure that hymns, prayers and the sermon can be understood and enjoyed by all ages attending
* we need to give young people opportunities for meaningful worship at other times (e.g. youth group devotions).

So what is worship?

The Uniting Church in Australia policy statement *Young People and Your Church* states the following about worship:

A meaningful worship life is crucial to all Christians young and old. If young people are to develop this meaningful worship life then they need to be involved in the church's Sunday worship services. It is important that they discover the meaning and disciplines of worship and that those who plan worship should ensure that worship invites all people including the young to participate actively.

It is important when planning worship to remember

* 'youth services' can be important but are second best to services which involve people of all ages together
* worship services of the church should relate to young people's hopes and needs and lives
* young people should be encouraged to attend and participate in the planning on a regular basis
* young people as well as adults can contribute meaningful leadership in worship in Bible reading, prayers, music, singing, banner making, drama...
* music is specially important to many young people and churches can plan with young people for some appropriate songs and music to be part of a congregation's worship
* young people should be encouraged to take worship beyond Sunday into their daily lives through the use of daily devotional material.

1. Define worship. Use WORK-SHEET 32 to look at some definitions of worship and then write your own.

2. Check the Bible. Look up each of these readings to see what the Bible says is involved in worship.
   Psalm 9:1-2
   Psalm 51:1-4, 9-12
   Philippians 1:3-8
   1 Corinthians 14:26

1 Corinthians 11:23-26
2 Corinthians 8:2, 5

3. Think through your own experiences of worship. Use WORKSHEET 33 to help you find out what makes worship meaningful for you.

4. Some visions for worship...

The following are based on a statement by the Rev. Dr Peter Horsfield, at the 10th anniversary of the Uniting Church, 1987.

I'd like to belong to a church where:
* Lay people share with the minister in the planning of services every Sunday. (Note: the minister is responsible for what happens in worship.)
* Every Sunday, worship:
  − is imaginative and creative
  − is rich with theological truth
  − includes not just words but also music, dance, rhythm, drama and colour.
* Members take responsibility for worship by:
  − coming each Sunday
  − getting adequate sleep the night before
  − arriving at church with a sense of awe and expectancy.
* People struggle to ensure that the ideas and language used in worship make sense, not only to people inside the church, but to people from outside the church as well.

The following are taken from the leaflet *The Church we Want* – an invitation to renewal from Australian young people of the Uniting Church, 1981.

- People are able to choose from a variety of worship patterns.
- The worship reflects biblical teaching and grows out of the life of the total church community.
- There is a joy and informality in worship while maintaining reverence.
- There is good music and song leadership, and variety in the songs sung, music played, musical instruments used and singing groups involved.
- What happens in worship is related to the rest of life and people are challenged.

Ways of helping young people understand worship

Use some of these activities with your young people.

* Attend a service as a group and make notes of things you appreciated or didn't appreciate, and words you didn't understand. Ask your minister to meet with you following the service.
* Have the young people interview members of the congregation on their way into the service, asking them why they have come and what they expect to get from the service.

Talk to the same people on the way out and ask them if worship fulfilled their expectations. Then have a discussion about people's expectations of worship.

* Visit worship services from other denominations and discuss the differences.
* Take some well-known hymns and examine the words. Try to re-write them in modern language.
* Ask your minister or an elder to come and speak on his/her understanding of worship.

How do we get young people involved in leading church worship?

How to get help with worship

Here are some models which could help parishes seeking to make their worship more participatory, creative and life filled. These models all involve the minister working with lay people each week in planning and leading worship. This has four major advantages.

a) It involves lay people in worship leadership.

b) It enables lay people to learn about worship from the minister.

c) It helps ensure that new, fresh ideas are being constantly generated.

d) It helps ensure that the worship grows out of the life of the church community.

NOTE: The minister is still responsible for what happens in worship.

Getting Help

1. Regular worship committees

Gather four (or more) teams of three people, who once a month will work with the minister to help him/her plan worship. The team should start with a Bible passage and work out the elements of worship from there.

2. Irregular worship committees

Gather four (or more) teams of three people, who once every two months will work with the minister to help him/her plan worship.

3. Worship helpers

Approach people to commit themselves to singly work with the minister to help plan and participate in worship each week (involving a different person each week on a roster basis). This would give the minister a person to 'bounce ideas off' and bring new ideas in. The people should be of a variety of ages, young, old, men, women, etc.

4. Worship groups

Invite groups, families, individuals to take responsibility for some of the elements of worship. For example, the minister might do the first part of the service and a family might take responsibility to present sermon, prayers, children's address. Or different groups might be asked to take responsibility for the majority of the elements in worship. The minister's job would be one of setting theme, providing resources, assisting the groups, and overall checking and co-ordination.

Things to note:
* The people asked to be involved need to be allowed to try some things out, so be prepared to take some calculated risks with content and be adventurous (within reason).
* There is no need for people to come with super-duper ideas every time.
* It is useful to introduce new things one at a time and slowly, so that people can get used to change. Some people will need help to accept different ways of worshipping.
* Put plenty of effort into the content. Don't try to disguise poor content with snappy presentation.
* Being creative does not mean being gimmicky. Those participating in planning should be reminded that they are helping people to worship God, not to be involved in a concert or 'me' centred hour of fun.

Use WORKSHEETS 34, 35, 36 to help with planning worship.

What are some creative worship ideas?

Creative planning can help make worship come alive for all ages. Don't plan something creative for the sake of simply being outrageous or gimmicky. When approached sensitively, creative elements encourage participation and help the biblical story become more real for us today. Creative worship also allows members of the congregation to express their gifts through music, drama, dance, art and writing.

If you want to try something new
– make sure that the minister and elders are supportive
– think through carefully what you want to do
– rehearse the segment in the church
– explain to the congregation what is happening during the service.

A. Readings

Always rehearse readings in the actual worship space with microphone (if to be used). Use people who can read effectively.

1) Reading with one or more readers – alternate verses or character parts.
2) Reading with congregational response – alternate verses (congregation united or in sections)
   – spoken echo
   – sung congregational response.
3) Reading with instrumental music as backing (piano or flute).
4) Reading with visual images (slides), candle.
5) Reading with drama or movement.

B. Drama

Again – always rehearse.

1) Depict the Bible story with a series of 'still' pictures using real people. Have the congregation open and close their eyes to see each picture as the story is read.
2) Dramatic monologue – character in costume telling the story in the first person.
3) Scripted plays.
4) Guided meditation – imagining the story with eyes closed.
5) Mime to reading.
6) Congregational response during a story (e.g. vocal sound effects).

C. Movement

1) Simple choreographed congregational movement to music.

2) Symbolic movement during prayer – kneeling, hands etc.

3) Mime/dance to reading and/or music.

4) Action songs.

D. Music

Always ensure that the words are visible, the melody line is audible and the songleader has a strong voice.

1) Sing an echo response e.g. sing a line of a psalm unaccompanied, congregation echoes back.

2) Sung chorus as a response to a spoken reading or prayer.

3) Write new words for a simple well known tune.

4) Use instrumental music with no words for meditation or to set the mood.

5) Use music with slides or dance.

E. Visual

1) Slides or pictures to illustrate intercessory prayer.

2) Banners.

3) Visual symbols – candles, bread, grapes, wheat.

4) Use of varied lighting – colour and intensity.

5) Slides with words and/or music as meditation.

Using symbols in worship

Preparation
1. Read the Scripture reading prayerfully several times.

2. Questions to ask yourself:
– What symbols are prominent in this story?
– What is the meaning of the symbol in the story?
– Is the symbol central or not?
– How could the symbol be represented visually, tangibly, or otherwise? Think of all five senses – sight, touch, taste, hearing, smell.
– How could the symbol be related to each element of the worship service? (Praise, confession, word, intercession etc.)
– How would the symbol relate to the overall tone of the worship – architecture, music, mood etc.?
– How will the symbol make the congregation feel – warm, uncomfortable, enlightened, confused, serious, funny?

Examples

Scripture	Story	Symbol
Exodus 3 & 4	God calls Moses	'holy ground' – special floor covering 'burning bush' – fire or light with cellophane 'stick' – walking stick
Ezekiel 37	Ezekiel's vision	dry bones
John 6	Bread of Life	fresh bread
Matthew 5	Salt and light	candles, lanterns
Acts 2	Pentecost	tape of rushing wind, fan with strips of cellophane and foil, red light
Matthew 13	Parable of sower	popcorn
Nehemiah		bricks and wall
Matthew 17	Transfiguration	mirror
John 15	True vine	grapes
John 13	Foot washing	basin, towel
John 4	Jesus at well	'well' with water
Luke 13	Mustard seed	seeds, cardboard leaves, 'tree'
Luke 10	Sending out 72	shoe inserts

Why should we have youth group devotions?

An important part of the program of any group for young people is the time when the whole group stops to worship God. This can take many different forms and amounts of time. One common worship time in youth group is the 5-15 minute devotion segment held at the beginning or end of the programmed activity. Another very popular idea, often used at camps, is to have a short time of complete silence in the evening. Following a short Christian input of some sort, campers are invited to use the next 10-15 minutes for private, silent reflection and prayer on the input, the day's activities or whatever they wish to reflect on.

NOTE: It is important to stress that 'reflection time' is a solitary time, that is, time spent by yourself. It is essential that there is no noise whatsoever, no radio, guitars etc. Campers may remain inside or go outside. A bell should be rung or music played when the time for silence is finished.

It's important to realise that not all members of a youth group will attend church worship regularly. Having devotions

* provides opportunities for young people to open their lives to God
* helps provide the group with a Christian focus
* encourages young people to develop a positive attitude toward worship in a relaxed environment
* provides teaching and biblical input which nurture young people in their faith
* allows young people to express their gifts and learn how to lead worship in a relaxed environment.

*** Why do you think devotions are important? ***

Devotions –
* Should to be a short act of worship, focusing on God.

* Should include prayer, biblical input, individual reflection, a challenge and an awareness of God.
* Should begin with something to settle the group down and have a clear starting point.
* Should relate the Bible to life issues.
* Should be short, sharp and punchy with a strong message.
* Should, if possible, relate to the theme of the youth group activity.

How do we plan devotions which are creative, relevant and challenging?

When planning a devotional or reflection input, firstly consider the theme of the activity or camp and think about what message on that theme you would like to put across. Then think of how you will do that. It is a good idea to try to relate the devotional to the everyday lives of the young people in your group. Consider a range of different communication methods and the type of group you are trying to communicate to, and try to ensure that the method of presentation and communication is appropriate. It is important to consider the various communication resources (books, slides, rock songs, tapes, newspapers, lighting etc.) that are available. However remember that often a simple reflection or devotional can have as much meaning as one using all the multi-media gimmicks.

Contents of devotions can vary, but every devotion should at least include input from the Bible which includes Bible readings, some explanation of how the reading relates to now, and some time for prayer.

Devotions should have a few basic components, that are essential for any devotions. These are:

1. Call to worship. A brief opening prayer, or time of silence which allows people to prepare for the time of devotion, and reminds them they are entering into a time of focusing on God. A song or two may follow this.

2. Biblical input. Readings from the Bible; a story based on a passage from the Bible; references to Bible passages etc.

3. Some exposition of the biblical input, which makes the point of the input, and relates the input to the lives of the young people. There need not be necessarily a spoken message.

4. A benediction, or time of prayer which finishes the time of worship.

The above is not an exhaustive list, and other components can be part of a devotion e.g. singing, other prayer time, stories, testimonies, silence, guided meditations, sharing.

It is important to note that there are many different ways of presenting the components of a devotion. They do not have to be presented verbally. Other methods or presentation include using tapes of songs or people speaking, slides, films, drama, mime, dance, puppets, posters, cartoons, jigsaws, reverse offering, etc. It is also good to try to find methods of presentation which allow young people to participate, such as group sharing time, open prayers, participants writing things down – one word prayers, singing appropriate songs, sculpting prayers, etc.

It is also important to consider how you will create the appropriate atmosphere for the devotion e.g. by going to a small room, using candles, showing a single slide, etc.

Planning

When planning a devotion, it is important to consider:

1. The age of the group you are planning for.

2. The needs and interests of the group.

3. The program that the devotion will be part of; the activities that the group will be doing before and after the devotion, the theme of the program etc.

4. The main point(s) you want to make.

5. The most appropriate ways to present the components of the devotion to communicate your main points to the group members, and to enable the group to worship God.

Use WORKSHEET 37 for a simple approach to planning devotions

Some tips to remember

1. Don't let devotions go too long. You should be able to judge. If the group gets restless, it is time to stop.

2. Don't make devotions too short (less than 5 minutes) or let people feel it's just 'token'.

3. Don't do all the talking yourself, but allow others to participate.

4. Do have the group sitting close together, on the same level.

5. Do use creative media, like music, role plays, pictures, film segments.

6. Do relate the devotions to real-life situations your kids are experiencing.

7. Do take time at the start to quieten people down and remind them it is a quiet time.

When planning reflection time at camp, refer to WORKSHEET 38 at the end of this chapter.

How do we make good use of music?

Music is an important part of young people's lives. Tapes and CD's, radio, video clips and movie soundtracks are a constant feature of their world.

Music magazines, rock concerts and rock star t-shirts are important in many young people's lifestyles. To understand where young people are at we must become familiar with their music and their favourite rock stars.

Music is also important in the church as a medium of worship. We are all aware of the tensions which exist between the adults and young people in their music preferences in worship. It's interesting to note that drums and stringed instruments, which we now associate with modern music, would have been used in church worship long before the piano or organ. Music can be a vital and enriching dimension of a parish's youth ministry.

Why do you think music is important to young people?

....
....
....
....
....

Why do you think music is important in worship?

....
....
....
....
....

Hymns and songs allow people to express their faith 'head' and 'heart' in worship by singing praises, confessions, and commitment to serve. Music allows participation by the whole congregation as well as the musicians.

As we sing we take in the words of others and make them our own, we express our praise directly to God.

Here are some practical guidelines for using music in worship.

1. Use both traditional hymns and modern songs as both are important for the church's life and worship. Hymns give us a link with the faith of those who have gone before, while songs and choruses give contemporary expression to that same faith.

2. Choose hymns or songs on the basis of what they say and how that fits the worship theme. Don't just pick something because it has a nice tune. Ask how this song will shape the direction of the worship service.

3. Also take account of the tempo and melody of the music and what kind of mood it sets – bright and happy, reflective. If you are singing a series of songs, choose songs of similar mood, or vary the mood gradually (rather than suddenly).

4. Make sure that everyone can see a copy of the words. Don't assume that everyone knows the song. Often new people feel left out because they don't know the group favourites.

5. Is it a new song? If so, take time to teach it. Have someone sing or play through the melody clearly, then the congregation sing it. Do this one or two lines at a time.

6. Use strong singers to lead the music. Most people need to hear a melody to be able to sing along. Try to have a melody instrument like a piano or flute and not just guitars.

7. Be aware that not all young people like to sing, especially 12-15 year old boys. Fun songs will get young people involved initially, whereas serious worship songs may turn them off. The words of the songs need to be something they can relate to and make their own. If words or phrases aren't intelligible, take time to explain them.

8. Percussion instruments can add rhythm to the music and allow reluctant singers a means of participation (tambourine, wood block, sticks, shakers).

9. Make sure all musicians can see a copy of the music, know the key signature, and have a list of songs in correct order.

10. If you have no musicians, there are plenty of tapes of choruses which you can sing along with. Alternatively find a musician who will put some accompaniment on tape for you.

11. In a worship service, choose songs which reflect a range of responses to God. As well as songs of praise there are songs of confession, dedication.

12. As a group activity you can take Scripture verses and write a simple tune to them, repeating key phrases if necessary. Use a well-known tune if you like.

13. Rap music can also be used. Play a backing track, and the leader 'raps' a line which the group echo.

14. It is essential that musicians rehearse before worship so that the music can flow smoothly.

* What do your young people think of the music in your youth group or worship service?

....

....

....

....

....

* What are some ways in which you'd like to see this music improved?

....

....

....

....

....

....

....

....

....

* What are some resources you'd need to make these improvements?

....

....

....

....

....

....

....

Some music resources

Songs from the Still Strange Land – JBCE

Sing Alleluia – Collins Dove

All Together Now and *All Together Again* – Lutheran Publishing House (Adelaide)

Songs of Praise, Songs of the Kingdom, Songs of the Nations – Scripture in Song

Praise and Worship Series – Resource Christian Music

Praise For All Seasons

Songs of the Vineyard – Mercy Music

WORKSHEET 32: How do you define 'worship'?

Here are some definitions of worship. Read them and place a tick against any which you especially like. (If you are working in a group, share your answers).

'The worship of the Christian Church should be like a party of which God is the host, and everyone is invited.'

'Worship is... to honour; to regard with extreme respect and devotion; to adore.'

'Worship is a drama in which we re-enact the story of God's saving love and learn our parts as players.'

'Worship is affirming that God is hope for the future, Lord of the present, Creator and Guide in the past.'

'Worship is the work of the whole people of God.'
(This is the meaning of the word 'liturgy'.)

'Worship is a deep encounter with God and with other people.'

'Worship is the offering of ourselves – all we are and all we have – in thanksgiving and dedication.'

'Worship can be serious, fun, fast, slow, loud, silent, close, lovely, sweet, bitter, nourishing, emptying, inward, outward, selfless, free, structured, prepared, spontaneous, conservative, radical.'

Now write your own definition.

Worship is ...

....

....

....

....

....

....

....

....

WORKSHEET 33: How meaningful is worship for me?

1. Describe an experience of church worship which was meaningful to you.

....

....

2. Identify the things that made this worship meaningful.

....

....

3. What do you think makes worship meaningful for young people?

....

....

4. What are the attitudes of young people in your church towards worship?

....

....

5. What are your visions for worship in your church?

I DREAM A CHURCH...

WORKSHEET 34: Principles for planning worship

Place a tick against the statements you agree with.

Place a question mark against the statements you disagree with or don't understand.

1. Worship should enable people to experience closeness to God and to one another – not alienate them.

2. Worship should have clear structure of preparation to worship, encounter with God and God's Word and response to God.

3. Worship should be the work of the people.

4. Worship should engage the whole person – physical, emotional, intellectual, spiritual (loving God with heart, mind and soul).

5. Worship should engage all the senses – sight, touch, hearing, taste, smell.

6. Worship must focus on the gathered people and the world in which we live.

7. Worship should draw on the church's rich traditions and be relevant to modern society, its language and concerns.

8. Worship should be a celebration, not a funeral.

9. Worship should be prayerfully prepared and Spirit-led.

10. Worship should blend the obvious and the symbolic; word and sacrament, truth and mystery.

11. Worship should be intergenerational (for all ages).

WORKSHEET 35: Planning worship – order of service

What's happening	Element of Worship
1. Why are we here? Greeting/welcome	Call to worship
2. Who are we worshipping? Why are we thankful?	Prayers of adoration and praise hymns
3. Have we been obedient to God? Is our relationship damaged?	Prayers of confession Declaration of forgiveness
4. What does God want to say to us?	Bible reading
5. How does God's Word apply to our lives?	Preaching of the Word
6. What do we believe?	Creed or affirmation of faith
7. How do we respond to God's goodness?	Offering
8. What we our concerns? How should we live in the world?	Prayers of the people (intercessions)
9. How can we express our oneness in Christ?	The Peace
10. How can we celebrate God's love?	Holy Communion
11. How should we then live?	Sending out (Word of mission) Blessing/benediction Dismissal

WORKSHEET 36: Worship planner

DATE OF WORSHIP SERVICE: / /   PLANNERS:..

THEME.. BIBLE READINGS:...

Elements of Worship (insert songs)	Activity	People responsible	Equipment materials needed
Setting up venue			
Greeting/welcome			
Prayers of adoration and praise			
Prayers of confession Declaration of forgiveness			
Bible readings			
Preaching of the Word			
Creed or affirmation of faith			
Offering			
Prayers of intercession			
The Peace			
Sending out			
Benediction			

How to work with young people. Copyright © 1991 The Joint Board of Christian Education.

WORKSHEET 37: A simple approach to planning devotions

STEPS	DETAILS	ACTIVITY	MATERIALS NEEDED
1. CALL TO WORSHIP A song, prayer, Bible verse, statement or silence to help people focus on God			
2. LIFE SITUATION Choose an everyday situation or concern relevant to your young people. (steps 2 and 3 may be swapped around).	Write issue here	Think of how to depict this – song, mime, video, photo, story, role play, slides	
3. BIBLE PASSAGE Choose a Bible passage which says something for that situation.	Write passage here	Think of a way to communicate this – reading, drama, mime	
4. APPLICATION Return to the life situation with some questions or answers raised by the biblical material	Write questions or points here	Think of a way to reflect on this – prayer, spoken message, role play, song, discussion	
5. RESPONSE Finish with a focus on how each person might respond to God in this situation – give individuals the freedom to choose their own response		Use a prayer, silence, song, written response	

How to work with young people. Copyright © 1991 The Joint Board of Christian Education.

WORKSHEET 38: Reflection time at camp

REFLECTION: a time to be alone, quiet and still

Every evening, after tea, there will be a period of reflection. This will consist of some Christian input, followed by 15 minutes of silence. At the end of 15 minutes, music will be played to signal the end of reflection, and you should return to the main hall.

Reflection time is for:

- being by yourself
- complete silence
- being still
- meditation
- prayer
- thinking
- looking at the stars
- observing nature
- listening to the sounds of the bush
- getting in touch with God

Reflection is not a time for talking, taking a shower, making noises, singing, playing games, shining torches around, listening to the radio, playing the guitar, walking around disturbing others.

For many campers, reflection is one of the most significant and important times of the whole camp.

Use this space to jot down anything that comes to you during reflection e.g. learnings, inspirations, thoughts, draw pictures, symbols, etc.

How to work with young people. Copyright © 1991 The Joint Board of Christian Education.

Chapter 10

Small church groups

Small church groups

Can youth ministry happen if our church has only a few young people? 143

What are the advantages of small youth groups? 143

How can we make the group a good experience? 144

We are so small – what can we do? 146

WORKSHEET 39: Small groups involved in worship 147

WORKSHEET 40: Worship suggestions 148

WORKSHEET 41: Suggestions for ministry within the congregation 149

WORKSHEET 42: Service suggestions 150

WORKSHEET 43: Friendship and fun suggestions 151

Can youth ministry happen if our church has only a few young people?

Youth ministry is often overlooked in many areas of Australia with clichés like:

There are not enough kids in our church.

The age range of young people is too wide.

Kids have to travel too far.

We haven't any leaders.

We can't go to the movies, roller skating or bowling.

There are too many other things on.

If we are serious about youth ministry then we will overcome negative attitudes and plan for youth ministry to occur in our churches and parishes in ways that are most appropriate to the local situation.

It is not only isolated churches in Australia that have few young people. There are many large cities and provincial towns that have churches with only a few young people as part of the family.

Your church may not have the numbers to fill a 45 seat bus for an outing, provide a large choir for a musical or fill a football team, but churches of all sizes are faced with ministering to small numbers of young people.

Youth ministry is more than providing a Friday night friendship and fun group. Youth ministry is living out and sharing the gospel with young people – ministering to their needs and the needs of their world.

We need to blow away the following myths:

Only small churches have small numbers of young people.

Great youth groups go bowling and skating in large buses.

Great youth groups play football matches with each other.

Great youth groups present an annual musical.

Youth ministry is something that happens Friday night in the church hall.

A big youth group is a better youth group.

Nothing works with a small youth group.

If a youth group is small then something must be wrong.

Small youth groups are insignificant.

The primary objective of a small youth group is to grow.

Every church needs a youth group.

What are the advantages of small groups?

Intimacy

It is easier to get to know the whole group and build on possibilities of real Christian community.

Community

Community can take place when young people and leaders plan for process and balance within a group.

Involvement

It is easier to involve everyone in a small group and assure them that they have a contribution to make.

Flexibility

Small groups can be flexible in terms of changing program, adapting to venues, working in with others.

Identity

It is easier to establish identity within a small group. When the group really comes to know each other, who they are, where they have come from, what the purpose of the group is, then some good things can happen.

Leadership

It is often easier to recruit leadership in terms of working with a smaller group and it's great to have both young people and adult leaders working together with the group.

There are disadvantages in terms of finding appropriate resources to assist the group in its development and program. It is often harder in terms of getting kids to meetings when they are totally dependent on parents for transport and distance is significant. There can be some problems with the wide age range and there are often many demands on young people, particularly in rural areas with sport and community affairs.

Don't give up

Rather than allow the disadvantages to dissuade us from any form of youth ministry taking place, press on.

1) Define your purpose and direction.

2) Select activities to carry out that purpose.

3) Have the resources that suggest both content and methods for exploring specific concerns and doing projects.

How can we go about it?

Join with other churches on an ecumenical basis

There may be other churches in your community saying the same thing about only having a few young people. Join with them. Plan to do it together.

Plan for activities that can be shared across age groups

There are many activities available for groups with a wide range of ages. Some activities are done together, others spill into peer groups for parts of the program.

Make the best of time slots

In some isolated situations it may be appropriate to have a group after school when parents come into the town for shopping. Maybe you can make better use of Sunday morning and have a worthwhile youth activity before or after worship to minimise travel time.

Work on leadership

See Chapter 4 – Leader Development

Make creative use of videos, local personalities, picnic spots etc.

Make the group time a quality time so that young people will look forward to coming back.

Advertise all that your group is doing with the whole community, inviting everyone to join.

How can we make the group a good experience?

Youth ministry is the task of the whole church which has a responsibility to provide a setting where kids are accepted and loved. In this setting they can ask the important questions of life and faith and find themselves and God.

The whole church needs to:

1) Offer love and acceptance. The whole church has the responsibility to get to know its young people as persons; their names, their interests, their hopes and their dreams.

2) Listen carefully when they talk. Make sure that young people are heard and encouraged.

3) Appreciate the skills they offer and encourage their gifts to be used in the life of the church and the community.

4) Provide opportunities for young people to spend large amounts of time with their peers doing a variety of interesting and fun activities.

5) Stand by them when they are difficult to love. They need acceptance, with their music, their dress, their attitudes.

6) Provide encouragement when they ask questions, when they do their thinking and when they search for meaning.

7) Offer Christ. The church needs to provide those opportunities through camps, worship, special sharing times when young people are given an opportunity to respond to Jesus Christ as a culmination of all of their growing and learning, that they may come through a significant experience to know a personal faith.

Young people are part of the church today. They need every opportunity to respond to that fact as they are exposed to the richness and diversity of the whole church and ultimately own the Christian faith for themselves.

What is needed to make a small group work?

1) Keep a positive attitude.

2) Do some long-range planning.

3) Don't try to compete with the supergroup in the city.

4) Never cancel an activity because of low attendance.

5) Choose a meeting space that fits your group.

6) Combine forces with other groups.

7) Participate in denominational and non-denominational events.

8) Incorporate your young people into the life of the church.

9) Don't ignore age difference.

10) Develop a philosophy of ministry independent of size.

REMEMBER

A group needs a purpose or sense of direction.

Advisers, young people, parents, and the church councils need to share a common vision of what the youth group is to be and do.

When the group plans, it can then select activities to carry out this purpose.

Steps in planning a youth group program

1) Set goals for the program.

2) Get your resources together in plenty of time so that the meeting can go smoothly.

3) Make sure the programs are relevant to young people and provide balance in terms of fun, study, fellowship and service.

4) Work hard on devotions and come up with discussions that involve all participants at a level they can cope with.

5) Spread the leadership load. Have as many people involved as possible and provide them with a sense of achievement.

6) Evaluate. With your key leaders, work over the things have gone well, the things that were just okay and the things that didn't work.

Keep programs balanced

Fellowship – opportunities for the kids to develop understandings of themselves, their friends, God, the church and the community.

Worship – opportunities to see and value God and respond at a level that is appropriate for them.

Study – provide opportunities for young people to grow in their understanding of the Scriptures, the church, the world and service.

Service – work hard to provide mission opportunities that the group might work on and develop a sense of really being a group as they serve other people within the congregation and within the wider work of the community.

We are so small – what can we do?

Plan ahead.

Work with the kids. Enable them to see that they are part of the total program of the church.

Work with the leaders. Dream dreams, set goals and aims that can be achieved.

Balance fellowship, worship, study and service.

Work on a 3 month plan for 12 meetings.

SAMPLE

1. a games night
plan for annual camp

2. share a video –
   Godspell
   Romero
   Dead Poets Society

3. study night
Jesus in Matthew, building on aspects from *Godspell*

4. Jesus in Matthew
   build on *Godspell*

5. Jesus in Matthew
build on *Godspell*

6. clowning night
learn about clown ministry : fun and serious things

7. plan for next week's worship service

8. worship service

9. camp weekend

10. camp reflection meeting

11. service project – day – church hall

12. music meeting – tapes that communicate.

Encourage the participants of the group to learn by doing, not only when they meet as a group but during the rest of the week.

Try and involve your young people in preparation and in the administration of each meeting.

Enable the group to work towards building community as you gently introduce your young people to
   what the church is and does
   why we worship
   the importance of the sacraments
   the basis of the faith
   confirmation.

Confirmation can be built into the general program of the group and the confirmation service can be a significant part of the program each year.

Use WORKSHEETS 39, 40, 41, 42, 43 to guide your planning in your particular local situation.

WORKSHEET 39: Small groups involved in worship

You don't need to have a large group to be involved in the worship life of
your church. The following list suggests some ways in which small groups
or individual young people can participate.

- During the regular worship service
  - Call to worship
  - Write and lead the prayers
  - Read the Bible
  - Prepare a drama
  - Prepare an audio-visual, etc.
  - Give the children's talk, puppets, drama, etc.
  - Select the music
  - Participate in playing music
  - Liturgical dance
  - Assist with greeting people.
- Special occasions – Christmas, Advent, Lent, Pentecost
  - Make an Advent wreath and light the candles during a service
  - Make decorations for a Christmas tree
  - Prepare a Passover meal
  - Paint and decorate eggs to share on Easter morning
  - Learn a new song and teach it to congregation
  - Use drama, puppets, dance, to share some aspect of the special
    occasion
  - Make banners on the theme
  - Decorate the church.
- If your church has a worship committee ask that a young person be
  involved on a regular basis. This could be different young people taking
  turns and participating as regularly as they can.

WORKSHEET 40: Worship suggestions

Use these suggestions to guide your planning for successful youth ministry in your local situation.

Agape meal/Agape feast (a worship experience designed around a meal)

Advent wreath lighting during worship service

Make decorations for Christmas tree

Children's talk

Christmas program

Conduct prayer service

Design and conduct worship at church picnic

Design and lead Sunday morning family service

Design and lead worship for day camp

Design and lead worship service for children

During Sunday morning service
  — Call to worship, Scripture
  — Prayers, offering
  — Mini-dramas
  — Use of audio-visuals
  — Puppets
  — Music, musical
  — Instrumental music
  — Role play
  — Dance
  — Act out parable
  — Usher

Easter sunrise service

Hymn of the month (youth research and publish information in bulletin or newsletter)

Lead worship for elderly

Lenten service

Live nativity scene

Make banners

New Year's Eve service

Outdoor worship

Palm procession

Passover

Prayer at congregational functions

Regular attendance

Visit other churches

Worship at retreats or camps

Worship in catacombs (simulating early Christians)

Worship workshop

Write hymns and songs (write words to familiar hymn or song tune)

Write on 3 x 5 cards thoughts or prayers for use in worship

Young people do entire service

Young people's choir

WORKSHEET 41: Suggestions for ministry within the congregation

Use these suggestions to guide your planning.

Adult/young people's bowling teams, volleyball, softball

Adult/young people's seminars on topics

Bake and serve biscuits after church (with all young people present – emphasis on visibility)

Big brother/big sister for children (young people are big brother or sister to individual small children of the church)

Car wash

Carol singing (either to members' homes or with adults)

Clean church yard

Design mini-course for children

Dramas

Easter egg hunt for children

Easter sunrise breakfast

Fun night or family night dinner (young people lead all activities; recreation; group building games; values exercises)

Help prepare Sunday school and kids club materials

Help with vacation day camp
  − teaching
  − recreation
  − music
  − refreshments
  − nursery for leaders' kids

Help with worship

Intergenerational study groups

Interview adult classes (with or without tape recorder)

Lead Advent workshops for children

Make banners

Make posters for various emphases
  − Christian education
  − Youth ministry

Make visual aids for teachers

Mission night (with meal of that country) and a speaker

New members assimilation (assign-a-young person)

Parent night/parent reception

Play instruments for accompaniment in worship

Present special programs or displays on study topics

Puppet show
  − have puppet workshop for young people
  − present show for children or for congregational dinner

Recreation and parties for children

Serve in the nursery group or creche

Sponsor special food collection (collect from congregation for local needy families)

Tape ministry for shut-ins and hospitalised

Team teaching in Sunday school

Ushers

Video presentation on church or Sunday school, or on seasons of the church year

Work with elderly and shut-ins
  − bake cakes
  − birthday cards, make gifts
  − make emergency telephone numbers book
  − adopt a grandma/pa
  − clean yards and odd jobs
  − run errands
  − take them shopping
  − telephone check-up

Young people's choir or band

Youth visit youth (a welcoming group for new young people)

WORKSHEET 42: Service suggestions

Use these suggestions to guide your planning.

Brainstorm ongoing service to elderly
- birthday cards
- writing letters for them
- singing
- checking (on telephone)
- doing errands
- taking them shopping

Christmas for prisoners – make stockings and fill with toothbrushes, soap, etc.

City cleanup

Clown ministry

Coffee house

Collect for church appeals (Care, Share, Lenten, etc.)

Craft projects to make gifts for elderly

Day camp in low-income neighbourhood

Education of community on social concerns by displays or presentation (connected to a study young people have done)

Food and clothing collection and distribution

Freedom from Hunger

Give program for senior citizens
- Christmas
- puppets
- any time

Help with city recreation program

Help with Meals on Wheels

Helping in library - Saturday reading program

Helping with girls' or boys' club

Invite non-church-related friends to activities

Neighbourhood cleanup

Parties or picnic for children's homes or disabled children's centre

Puppet shows for children

Recycling paper and aluminium cans

Singing for convalescent homes

Sponsor needy families

Summer program for pre-schoolers in low-income neighbourhood

Take care of lawns for elderly

Toys for poor at Christmas

Tutoring

Visits in day-care centres

Work camps

WORSHEET 43: Friendship and fun suggestions

Use these suggestions to guide your planning for effective youth ministry in your local situation.

Barbecue
Beach
Bicycling
Bowling
Camping
Camps
Camps with other church youth groups
Canoe trips
Car caravans
Carnival
Carol singing
Coffee house
Cold (rough) camping
Community cultural events
Cook dinner for parents
Crab soccer
Craft projects
Craft workshops
Dances
Denominational youth conferences (synod, presbytery, district, association)
District camps
Eat out (burger or pizza place)
Group building activities
Hay rides
Hikes
Horseback riding
Jogging
Lock-ins (sleep-ins)
Mimes
Miniature golf
Mission night
Museums
Parties
Polaroid scavenger hunt

Pool
Progressive dinners
Rafting
Recreation (games)
Refreshments in homes
Rock concerts
Sailing
Scavenger hunt
Singing
Skating
Snow skiing
Sports
   — with other groups
   — baseball
   — cricket
   — softball
   — tennis
   — volleyball
   — soccer
   — basketball
   — football
Square dance or bush dance
Swimming
Table tennis
Talent show
Television viewing
This Is Your Life
Trips
Values mini-course
Videos
Water skiing
Work camps
Young people's singing groups
Young people's rallies

Chapter 11

Evangelism

Evangelism

What is evangelism?   155

How can we get our church interested in evangelism to young people?   155

What are some ways of reaching out to young people?   156

How can we help young people share their faith?   158

How can the local church and youth groups be open to new people?   159

How can we give young people opportunities to make faith commitments?   160

WORKSHEET 44: Witnessing   162

What is evangelism?

Evangelism is a 'church' word! KIDS DON'T USE IT in their normal vocabulary.

It is the Good News of the Gospels, the written accounts of the good news that God has acted in history through the life, death and resurrection of Jesus. It calls for a response from people today.

The Uniting Church in Australia policy statement *Young People and Your Church* says the following about reaching out and evangelising with young people.

Evangelism

Christian people have a special privilege and responsibility to pass on the good news of Jesus Christ to people of all ages. Young people need to hear and see the relevance of the life changing potential of the gospel. Every church is called to explore different ways of challenging and inviting young people to be disciples of Christ. This can happen through

- helping young people to own and share their faith through confirmation training and participation in small discipleship groups
- helping young people to understand that the most effective ways of evangelising are through friendship and relationships which have integrity; e.g. caring for, listening to, sharing faith, just being with people
- running evangelistic events such as coffee shops, concerts, visiting secondary schools...
- using a variety of methods to communicate the gospel e.g. music, dance, drama...

Young people in the community

The church must follow the command and example of Jesus and reach out to all people. This means outreach to young people in the community and not just the young people in the church. The youth work of a church should include being with young people

- in the schools, clubs, unemployment centres, tertiary institutions, streets of local communities...
- who are unemployed, on drugs, caught up in family problems, isolated and alone...

The programs may be drop in centres, action for justice, evangelism, self-help projects, camps, or just being there. A church cannot do everything. But if it is doing nothing to express God's love for young people in the community there is something seriously wrong.

How can we get our church interested in evangelism to young people?

Church history in Australia over the past 40 years has shown that it is often young people who have had to struggle with this question. Evangelism is the task of the whole church, the community of God's people, but as the church becomes institutionalised and finds itself in a maintenance mould the tasks and opportunities of evangelism are forgotten and put on the back burner.

Often it is young people who remind the church of its prime task.

Evangelism must always be seen as the work of the whole church, the community of God's faithful people. We miss the point if we talk about evangelism being 'my work' or the work of the young people, the cell group or the evangelism and outreach committees.

Leadership within the youth ministry area in a local congregation should see itself as working along with the ministry team and other agencies of the life of the church in a number of settings. They have a responsibility within the youth ministry setting. The sharing of God's Good News and giving opportunity for a response to that Good News needs to be worked at in the youth group, in the Sunday morning programs, through worship and in the modelling and credibility building that leaders do with young people within the life of the church.

There is opportunity within the congregation for young people to integrate and share their ideals and enthusiasms for evangelism and mission by being involved in worship, by participating in organisations and governing bodies within the life of the church at the local level.

Opportunities always exist within the immediate community surrounding the life of the church building. Shopping centres, coffee shops, indoor parlours, sporting groups, recreational facilities, parks, are all meeting places where the presence of the gospel should be seen and heard.

Most churches offer opportunity for young people to become involved in regional, presbytery, state and national events. Conventions, mission projects, overseas exchanges, training seminars are opportunities for young people to receive and also give as they share in understanding evangelism.

What are some ways of reaching out to young people?

Your congregational youth ministry team should see evangelism as one of its specific goals for the year. It is important that the committee identifies particular issues, situations and needs in your area and works from them and towards them.

Use WORKSHEET 44 at the end of this chapter to help your understanding and planning.

Witnessing in the culture

'Evangelism is a personal invitation to become a part of God's Kingdom. Not only to belong to it but to help build it and make it a reality on earth.' *Reaching Youth Today : Heirs to the Whirlwind* by Barbara Hargrave and Stephen D. Jones.

Young people are people in cultures. Becoming a Christian will have more influence if we enable people to work out their faith through their culture.

Some try and create a Christian culture by removing themselves from their surrounding culture.

e.g. Christian schools, Christian radio stations, T.V. stations, Christian business directions, perhaps even Christian music, drama, books, etc.

Three steps in cultural outreach

1. Identify the culture – dress, eating habits, housing, social norms, cultural images, belief, values or what is socially learnt and shared by a group of people.

2. Identify the redeemable Christ likeness in the culture.

3. Find ways the faith may be expressed through the culture.

This third step is what we may refer to as nurture. The method of concrete communication or nurture Jesus used may be described in four steps.
1. I speak: you listen
2. I do: you watch
3. You do: I watch
4. You do and report back to me.
In most cultures people will see the gospel before they listen to it. The most effective evangelism is

when people live with Christians and build up a long term relationship with them. That is friendship. 'Don't tell me I've got a friend in Jesus until you've shown me the friend that I've got in you.'
– Ken Medema.

Sometimes in a very short space of time people will pick up what you are saying and are on about. Even so it still needs building upon. The major foundation of youth ministry is relationships – or in other words it is –
'Like one beggar telling another beggar where to find bread.'
– D.T. Niles.

Being authentic is one of the most effective traits for getting the message across.

Some possibilities
* Go where people are:
a) Concerts
b) Pub
c) Amusement centres
d) Discos and dances
e) Parties
f) Hangouts e.g. milk bars, malls.
g) Sporting clubs

h)...

i)...

j)...

k)...

In other words don't hide away in Christian ghettos.

* Invite people to:
a) Go to a camp or trip with you (and/or others)
b) Functions the church is holding (if appropriate)
c) Home for a meal
d) Home

e) ....

f) ....

g) ....

h) ....

Getting the message across

These passages from the Bible can give you a thought provoking way of examining how effective we are in getting the message across. They could provide a valuable tool for your group to work through.

Biblical basis

Matthew 5:13-16 'You are like salt for all people. But if salt loses its saltiness there is no way to make it salty again. It has become worthless, so it is thrown out and people tramp on it.

You are like light for the whole world. A city built on a hill cannot be hidden. No-one lights a lamp and puts it under a bowl; instead he put it on a lampstand, where it gives light for everyone in the house. In the same way your light must shine before people, so that they will see the good things you do and praise your Father in heaven.'

Colossians 4:5-6 'Be wise in the way you act towards those who are not believers, making good use of every opportunity you have. Your speech should always be pleasant and interesting, and you should know how to give the right answer to everyone.'

1 Peter 2:12 'Your conduct among the heathen should be so good that when they accuse you of being evildoers, they will have to recognise your good deeds and so praise God on the Day of his coming.'

1 Peter 3:15 'But have reverence for Christ in your hearts, and honour him as Lord. Be ready at all times to answer anyone who asks you to explain the hope you have in you...'

'The church is the only organisation that exists for the benefit of its non-members.'
– Archbishop Temple.

'The church does not have evangelism as a minor part of its being. The church exists for evangelism.'
– George Morris.

We need to know why we are a Christian. Why we believe. Why do you believe? We need to know what we believe. If we do not know the story, what we will share? (Luke 24:25-27, Acts 8:27-31).

What is your story?

We need to know how to communicate it.

In Acts 17:16-24 what were some of the principles Paul showed or used?

Interpreting our context for communication

To whom are you communicating – know your context.

What are their images of
– God?
– faith?
– Christians?
– church?

What are their presuppositions?
* They need to know their need for God – If Jesus is the answer what are the questions?

Discover their culture
– music
– films
– T.V.
– interests
– humour
– worldview
– heroes

Find out what the basic questions are
– supernatural
– future
– death
– the individual
– the meaning of life
– values
– truth
– love
– suffering
– evil

* What is it in what they think and feel that are the doors or openings to the gospel? What are the spiritual questions?
* We use the word pre-evangelism which means the process of helping a person to open up to the gospel. A part of this is the ministry of apologetics which is giving an explanation of the faith.
* What are the questions you hear young people asking?
* Sometimes young people ask questions that they are not so much looking for answers for, but are search statements that they just need to get out before they will listen to what you have to say.
* Evangelism is not something we do to young people but rather, with them.

How can we help young people share their faith?

Ultimately faith sharing, witnessing, evangelism spring from a motivation and conviction that God has touched our lives and that experience of Christ has been so significant that above all else we want to share it with other people.

For this to happen a number of factors must be involved and young people must continually be encouraged in the task and equipped with tools that will assist their natural enthusiasm.

1. Understanding the Christian message

Opportunity needs to be given for people to understand what is the Christian message, contained in the Scriptures, and as the living word of God revealed to men and women and young people down through the ages. This message is shared when we have personally experienced the Christian good news so that the balance of Scripture, history and experience work together.

2. Understanding ourselves

We need to understand ourselves psychologically and understand ourselves spiritually to be equipped to share effectively.

3. Understanding others

If young people are going to communicate the faith then they also need to understand other people. Teaching in the Christian understanding of God's dealings with men and women must be given; also instruction on how to understand young people as they live in a changing world and are very much caught up with peer pressure and those changes.

4. Understanding ways we communicate our faith

Time and study need to be given to learning to live a Christian lifestyle; how to listen; how to really see people; how to pray; how to live under the leadership of the Holy Spirit our helper.

5. Learning to listen

This is a major component in communicating the faith and in direct opposition to many who think it's just a matter of remembering a number of texts and being able to push them out at the appropriate moment.

6. The role of the Holy Spirit

It is the Holy Spirit who brings people to God and directs that any gifts of the Spirit in their lives be reflected through the fruits of the Spirit. You may like to work through Galatians 5:22, 23 and take each word describing the 'fruits of the Spirit' and discuss the ways that the fruits of the Spirit make effective the communication of our faith to others.

Similarly your group may like to work on 1 Corinthians chapter 12 and seek to identify the gifts of the Holy Spirit listed in this chapter. Match them up with what is happening in terms of the life of the group and its members. It would be important to conclude the study by reading 1 Corinthians 13 and remembering that love overrides all else.

How can the local church and youth groups be open to new people?

If we are obedient to the claims of Christ and his teaching on lifestyle – that is, sharing our lives and building community, which involves caring, service and justice, then we will use a number of avenues to reach out with the Good News.

The following are a number of possibilities as recorded by a group of very intentional Christian young people at work in Australia in recent years.

1. Catalyst centres

Places of positive Christian training and experimental evangelism. Places working for the reconciliation of secular twentieth century psychology, literature, art, politics, and commerce with biblical Christianity. This may be for a tertiary institution, a community centre, or even a small group.

2. Through communities

The depersonalisation of our present society may be countered by providing drop-in centres and the development of Christian communities.

3. Through literature

Magazines, broadsheets and papers keeping a Christian word in a post Christian world.

4. In depth caring and social help

Christian social workers living on much less than they could earn elsewhere by giving their talents to the work of the faith.

5. Market place evangelism

At work, on the streets, in the universities and schools getting the gospel where it ought to be – out where the people are.

6. In creative arts

Aiming to show people new ways of expressing their beliefs by discovering their own potential creativity through music, dance, painting, silk screening, pottery, jewellery making etc.

7. In youth sub-cultures

Amongst the bikies, the surfers, the street kids, especially those not reached by the church now.

8. In media

The pilgrim people of Australia have not started to capitalise on the penetration of the media. We can't afford our own programs but other agencies can use our talents.

EXERCISE

Use this list as a conversation starter with your leadership team.

a) Identify from the above list the areas that you think your group could be involved in.

b) List those that you think are unrealistic.

c) Add to the list areas which you believe your group could pioneer.

How can we give young people opportunities to make faith commitments?

So often the cry comes 'We never challenge our young people to commitment!' 'Why doesn't our church make a clear call to commitment?' 'Why is it only when we go to big rallies or camps that there is an opportunity for young people to become Christians?'

These are real questions and have been asked of local churches for the last 40 years. Many people will embrace the faith as they grow up and are loved and accepted within the life of a local church. For others having grown up in the church there may be a 'Damascus road' experience where suddenly God breaks into their lives in a new and vibrant way and directions are changed as they were with Paul in Acts 9.

The church through its outreach must be prepared for young people who have no background in the faith to be touched by God's Spirit as they are challenged to make faith commitments. There are many appropriate and authentic opportunities that can be made for young people to respond to the faith. Some may be gentle, others may need to be strong and direct.

a) At a communion service

Opportunity can be given for people to acknowledge a special need for prayers or commitment in their lives and whilst communion is being distributed they can remain at the communion rail for prayers, conversation and counselling.

b) Guest services

Many churches have services once a month where young people are invited to bring friends and guests. In an appropriate and authentic way the gospel message is proclaimed. Opportunity can be given for response privately by talking to a friend, ministers, elders and youth leaders after the service.

c) In small groups

There will often be opportunity within a small group series for the small group or cell group to look at various aspects of Christian commitment relating to spiritual life, stewardship of money, time. Within the small group opportunity can be given for people to verbalise their feelings and share prayers for each other.

d) Youth camps and conventions

A good proportion of adult Christians in Australia today have made some act of commitment at an Easter Camp or at a National Christian Youth Convention. These are often times when sharing Christian community can give evidence to the possibilities of people living out their faith following an actual faith commitment, either within a small group, a small community, or the context of the whole camp or convention.

e) One to one opportunities

Ministers, elders and leaders need to accept the fact that there will be 'God moments' in the lives of their young people through various circumstances (change of direction, bereavement, exam results, relationship breakdown, parents' divorce etc.) when they will be particularly open to God and claims on their lives.

Those moments need to be seized and sometimes young people need to be pointed in the right direction. Perhaps over a cup of coffee or walk on the beach, opportunity can be made for conversation about commitment for prayer and counselling.

f) Vocation situations

Many young people, as they are looking to the future in terms of vocation, are open to questions such as 'Where do you think God is leading you in these circumstances?' or 'Where do you see God's hand in your future?' From natural situations like these, positive conversation about faith commitment can follow.

g) Relationships

The development of boy-girl relationships, engagement, preparation for marriage, the break down of relationships and even the break down of marriage can be opportunities where ministers, elders and leaders can talk to their young people about faith commitments.

h) Sports nights

Have a hands-on or demonstration sports night inviting key Christian sports persons to be involved, asking them at an appropriate time during the evening to share their faith experiences.

i) Music concerts

Opportunities exist to let music tell the story. A number of methods could be used to give opportunity for a Christian response.

j) ....
....
....
....
....
....

k) ....
....
....
....
....
....

EXERCISE

Brainstorm amongst your leaders and be open for other ideas and possibilities to fill in j) and k).

Wholistic approach

It is important that faith commitments are not made on the basis of emotion alone or that opportunities for faith commitments are only given once a year at an emotional time.

Strong leadership should be given to enable faith commitments to be made in the context of the faith community with adequate opportunity for the intellect, the emotions and the will to be exercised.

The opportunity for faith commitments within worship, small groups, or on a one to one basis should be made often, with sensitivity and strength. Remember at all times that it is God who brings people to commitment through the work of the Holy Spirit in the lives of men, women and young people.

Statement of evangelism

by Dr. George Morris

'To evangelise is the proclamation by word and deed of God's works of salvation in Jesus Christ. Its intent is changed lives and renewed relationships which demonstrates the love, peace, and justice of the Kingdom of God. Its means are not coercion, fear or glib commercialism, but humble witness, patience, and firm reliance on the power of God's Spirit to transform the sharing of our faith into personal whole life commitment. Its scope includes the commissioning of every believer to move outward in love to family, friends, neighbours and strangers. Its role in the church is essential as the primary response to unconditional love, and its necessity for today cannot be exaggerated.'

WORKSHEET 44: Witnessing

READ AND THINK ABOUT

a) 'But the lord said to me, "Do not say that you are too young, but go to the people I send you to, and tell them everything I command you to say. Do not be afraid of them, for I will be with you to protect you. I the Lord, have spoken!"'
(God, speaking to young Jeremiah – Jeremiah 1:7-8)

b) While we must take seriously the sociological phenomenon known as adolescence, there can be no justification for a separate youth church which neither makes the contribution to, or draws its strength from the ongoing life of all God's people. The way young people are recognised as part of the body will have a marked impact on effectiveness of our witness to the gospel of reconciliation.

NOW COMPLETE

1. Are youth involved in the witness and outreach of your congregation/parish?   YES NO

2. Rate this involvement on a scale of 1-10. (1 indicates very little involvement and 10 indicates extensive and meaningful involvement.)

1	5	10

3. In what ways are young people involved?

☐ assist in planning for congregation outreach and evangelism

☐ visiting with a minister or elder

☐ contribute to church bulletins or newsletters

☐ serve by greeting people at the door before worship

☐ participate in evangelism training programs

☐ by personal evangelism

☐ other (specify)...

4. What one activity (not ticked in Q3 above) could you undertake to increase the involvement of your young people in the witness and outreach of your congregation/parish?

Chapter 12

Social issues

Social issues

Youth ministry and social issues   165

Issues affecting young people   166

Why should young people be involved in outreach to the community?   167

How can we get young people interested in outreach and social issues?   167

What are some ways of getting young people involved in outreach?   168

Who else is involved in community and global issues?   171

WORKSHEET 45: Justice in the time of Amos   172

WORKSHEET 46: Interest or apathy   173

Youth ministry and social issues

We live at a time when some people have turned Christianity into a very private personal experience. They want to experience God in their lives and to build close relationships with other Christians like themselves. But they steer away from becoming involved in social issues – especially issues involving economic and political action.

This understanding of the Christian faith leads to youth ministry which is about fellowship and private and personal experience and church group activities.

What is left out are some of the most important parts of the gospel and large and vital aspects of the message of the Bible.

The message of many of the prophets in the Old Testament was against 'being religious' but not taking action to respond to people's needs and to bring justice into their country.

See for example:
Amos 5:7-15; 5:21-24
Micah 6:6-8

Jesus by both his example and his teachings directed his followers to care deeply about what happened to people, particularly the poor and those oppressed by society. He taught his disciples to pray and work for the will of God to be done on earth.

See for example:
Matthew 9:10-13
Matthew 23:23-24
Matthew 25:31-46

To be involved in social issues is therefore not an option for youth ministry; it is necessary if we are to look at the world through the eyes of Christ and to share in God's mission in the world.

There are two big implications for youth ministry:

- the kind of young people we think of as included in youth ministry.
- what young people in our youth ministry programs are challenged about and equipped to take action on.

The policy statement *Young People and Your Church* put the issues very clearly:

Young people in the community

The church must follow the command and example of Jesus and reach out to all people. This means outreach to young people in the community and not just to the young people in the church. The youth work of a church should include being with young people:

- in the schools, clubs, unemployment centres, tertiary institutions, streets of local communities...
- who are unemployed, on drugs, caught up in family problems, isolated and alone.

The programs may be drop in centres, action for justice, evangelism, self-help projects, camps, or just being there. A church cannot do everything. But if it is doing nothing to express God's love for young people in the community there is something seriously wrong.

Young people and Your Church
Uniting Church Press, Melbourne
1989, page 8

Issues affecting young people

The process of changing from a child to an adult is a complex one in our society. Even under good conditions in family, school and work, young people can run into problems such as:

- tension with parents
- finding suitable accommodation
- coping with school
- selecting a job
- deciding about use of alcohol
- deciding about drugs
- understanding options for sexual behaviour.

However in recent years, changes in society have increased the pressures on some young people so that particular issues have fresh urgency and some new issues affect many young people. Some of these issues are:

- homelessness
- unemployment
- sexually transmitted diseases
- drug abuse
- AIDS
- attitudes to homosexuals and lesbians
- adequate health care
- equal opportunities for young women
- equal opportunities for young people and ethnic groups.

These issues are reflected in our newspapers and on our television screens. For the youth ministry of your church to be effective you need to know what the particular needs of young people are in your area. Finding out about these often involves more than just planning for a youth group to meet. A church needs a small group of people to find out about local needs. This involves talking to different kinds of people in the community – members of the church, parents of teenagers, young people, teachers in local schools, the staff of agencies involved in meeting community needs, social workers linked with the City Council or Shire, and so on.

A group working on this task does not have to be a permanent committee. Even a short term task group can find out enough to get any church started on doing something about ministry to young people in the community.

The Action Manual accompanying the policy statement *Young People and Your Church* puts it this way:

- What ways of reaching out to young people in a community is your church now involved in?
- What are some of the big needs of young people in your area?
- How can the church start consideration of some new possibilities for meeting youth needs in your area?
- What are other churches or agencies in the community doing? Would it be constructive to offer to work cooperatively in meeting youth needs?

Young People and Your Church Action Manual Uniting Church Press Melbourne 1989, page 24

This kind of youth ministry requires a support base in your church. Take a description of needs and proposals for possible action to the Council of Elders and ask for support from the church as a whole. Youth ministry is the whole church serving young people in the name of Christ. It involves more than just appointing leaders to youth groups, though that is important.

This kind of youth ministry is often best carried out in partnership with other agencies in the community – schools, other churches, and community organisations. So reach across barriers of denomination and organisation to form coalitions for effective service to young people in the community.

Why should young people be involved in outreach to the community?

Involving young people in service to other young people is a part of a church's response to youth needs. It is also a way of discovering more about the Christian faith.

The Bible is full of references to serving others and working for justice. The Bible can be seen as a guide to how we live our lives. If this is so, then prayerfully serving others and being just is a high priority

The book of Amos is one guide to what God requires of people and the way we are expected to behave.

Use WORKSHEET 45 to compare the time of Amos with society today.

The example of Jesus' life is powerful. When you read about the people he associated with, the caring, healing, liberating and fair ministry he exhibited, you cannot escape the message of justice.

How can we get young people interested in outreach and social issues?

Service and social issues should be an important part of the life of any church group. Serving others and working for justice are fundamental parts of the Christian faith. Service and social issues activities in a group for young people should make the participants aware of the needs of others, and allow them to demonstrate in a practical way their concern.

NOTE: In serving others, we find some of our own needs are met by those we serve. There is no fixed giver-receiver relationship or one way teacher-learner relationship.

Ten principles for youth group service and social issues projects and activities

Try to choose projects and activities which

1. both serve others and work for social justice;

2. involve your whole group, and have the potential to be group building (it's okay to have fun too – people are more likely to get involved if they are meeting people and enjoying themselves too);

3. are within the capacities of your group to achieve;

4. have an educational component as well as action;

5. enable your young people to learn about the project by doing it (then reflecting on what they've learnt);

6. are ongoing and can be done by your group on a regular basis;

7. enable your group to work at the level of helping individuals or groups as well as working for social or political change; (You may have a range of different projects/activities aimed at different levels.)

8. enable your group to give of themselves, i.e. their time, effort, money, emotions etc.;

9. enable your group to interact with the lives of other people;

10. have the potential to help your group change and grow in Christian discipleship as appropriate to both the people being served and the people serving.

NOTE: Let prayer undergird all that you do, and regularly review what you do in service and social justice.

What are some ways of getting young people involved in outreach?

23 ways to build social awareness in youth ministry

The most important thing is to make social issues a regular part of your youth ministry program.

1. Study justice readings in the Bible e.g. Amos, Jeremiah, the Sermon on the Mount, etc.

2. Study social issues in your friendship and fun groups or discipleship groups e.g. Bible studies, topical issues of the day.

3. Join Amnesty International as a group and regularly write letters.

4. Get yourself and/or your group on the mailing list of your church's social justice division, mission division, etc.

5. Attend the Palm Sunday peace march and other appropriate demonstrations as a group.

6. Pray about social issues in your groups.

7. Subscribe to social justice magazines:
   Sojourners: P.O. Box 29272, Washington DC 20017
   New Internationalist: P.O. Box 82, Fitzroy 3065 Ph: (03) 419 7111
   Outlook: P.O. Box 2134, Sydney NSW 2001 Ph: (02) 264 3669
   Australian Society: 88 King William St., Fitzroy Vic 3065

8. Buy and read books on social issues e.g. *You Can Do It – Overcoming Youth Unemployment* by Daddow and Grierson; *The Cry of the People* by Penny Lernoux.

9. Encourage your young people to travel overseas, but especially to Third World countries, not just as tourists but to meet the people and look, listen and understand.

10. Have regular service tasks that your young people do, especially tasks which involve face to face contact with another group of people e.g. relieve at the local house for homeless kids.

11. Pick one social issue each year, and make it your group's project for the year to study the issue. Have speakers on the issue, raise money, write letters, take other action.

12. Use simulation games which help your young people to get to a feelings level on social issues e.g. Zinga; Arms Race; Break Down the Walls; Unequal Resources; Poverty. (These and more can be found in *Simulation Games 1, 2, 3*, available from The Joint Board of Christian Education, Melbourne, or your nearest Christian book supplier.)

13. Arrange for young people from your church to live for a week with a church family from a socially and economically deprived area.

14. Celebrate Social Justice Sunday in your parish.

15. Agitate for your parish to form a social justice committee including some young people, or lobby to get some young people on the social justice committee if you already have one.

16. Visit the offices of your church's social justice division; State Council of Churches; Mission Office; Amnesty Office etc., and look at their resources. Buy those that seem most relevant to you.

17. Show films or videos on social issues to your groups e.g. *If You Love This Planet; Missing; Under Fire; Threads; The Day After; A Glad House; Cry Freedom; The Other Facts of Life*; 'Minutes to Midnight' – audio visual.

18. Arrange for appropriate speakers to visit your group.

19. Link up with community organisations that are working on issues that you are interested in.

20. Go as a group to hear speakers on social issues, especially those from interstate or overseas.

21. Become members of social justice programs run by the church e.g. peace registers, or campaigns that offer a chance to share resources.

22. Link up with the Aboriginal groups in your area, and see how you can work with them on issues.

23. Celebrate 'One World Week' (usually September or October) in your parish.

Use WORKSHEET 46 with your group to discover the current social concerns of your young people.

Developing social justice initiatives

1. Start with yourself

Ask yourself what are your own concerns? what do you have difficulty with? what worries you personally?

The troubles you face as an individual may give you an insight on wider social problems. Many individual traumas and troubles have later been identified as social problems and social injustices – for example, work discrimination against women, hardships caused by tax laws, divorce laws, abortion laws, homosexuality, the poor.

2. Share

Share your concerns and insights with others in your group. Find out if they have similar concerns or suffer the same worries or difficulties. Listen to others tell of their concerns, reflect on whether you share their perceptions. Discuss with the group which of their concerns may be serious issues for the local community.

3. An option for the poor

The first thing for the group to do is to ask:'Who are the people at the bottom of the heap on this issue?' 'Who are the powerless and voiceless?' 'Who are the people who have no grounds for hope?' In this way the poor are identified. The group then finds out what is their perception of the problem, and what sort of things they would like the group to do to help. If this enquiry is not to be patronising or even destructive it is vital for group members to be very humble and attentive to what is being said. It is a spiritual discipline that is applicable equally to international or domestic issues.

4. Working with others

Contact with others is particularly important when you are tackling a local issue. The only way to understand what's happening is to meet as many people who are involved as possible. This includes local community organisations and political groups. You may have reservations about some of their views, but that is no excuse for not working with them. Christians must co-operate with all people of goodwill in trying to establish God's reign of justice, love and peace.

5. See – Judge – Act – Evaluate

See...

Seeing things from the point of view of the poor takes an effort. Their point of view is only rarely put on television or in the press. Material from the church's justice divisions try to compensate for this bias.

Other useful journals/publications include:
Australian Society
Sojourners
New Internationalist

Listen to other people's stories. The newspapers are full of people's concerns, but often their stories are incomplete. Many peoples' stories are not newsworthy and never get into print. We need to listen to those in our community whose voices are rarely heard – the poor, oppressed, the powerless, the people facing the problems.

Listening to these people may involve more than just a speaker at a church meeting. There needs to be some regular contact and involvement. Often it is important to meet with local groups in ways and places where they feel confident and assured.

Judge...

Try to pick out aspects of the problem your group might tackle locally. Is there someone with special knowledge? Is one of the problems of particular local concern? What local activities are there which your group should support?

Act...

Divide the problem into clear issues, the issues into sub-issues, and the sub-issues into manageable bits.

How to plan action that succeeds

The golden rule is to take a general problem, cut from it a recognisable issue, break this into realistic sub-issues, and then mount actions on the sub-issues. This is followed by evaluation and celebration.

The problem

Take a general problem. A group cannot tackle something like the isolation of the elderly or the exploitation of plantation workers in general. That is too woolly. The first task is to cut an issue out of the general problem.

The issue

This begins to look more manageable. But it still needs to be focused, and broken into sub-issues which can be dealt with one at a time.

Sub-issues

The group now has to decide on which sub-issues can it realistically act. It must break down the sub-issues into a number of distinct actions, i.e. work out an action plan.

Success, evaluation and celebration

Finally there is time for evaluation and celebration.

Some examples

1. A younger member of a church went to Korea to work in the Seoul Urban Industrial Mission, where there are many problems of poverty and injustice. Through slides and speakers at a couple of events for young people, the group was informed of the work the young missionary was involved in, and the help needed. The group decided to work to raise funds to help the missionary as a show of support to him in his work. The fund raising events undertaken, were a 'Generation Gap' dance for the whole Parish, and a film night.

2. Members of a group became concerned about the needs of young Asian immigrants. The local hostel was contacted and it was decided to invite young people from the hostel to an evening organised by the group. The evening took the form of a mixing games night which helped the Vietnamese young people meet informally some Australian young people, (and vice-versa). It was an enjoyable and worthwhile event for all. It would have been better if ongoing contact with the hostel had been continued.

A similar event was organised for young people with physical disabilities from a local social health centre. These young people were invited to join in further meetings, where appropriate.

3. The youth group takes responsibility for doorknocking an area for Community Aid Abroad doorknocks each year. Doorknocking is a task which few people enjoy, even while recognising the worth of the task. Therefore, the doorknocks are often preceded by a lunch together at the hall, or afternoon tea at the hall or someone's place after it is finished. This introduces a social, fun aspect to the doorknock and encourages more participants.

4. A group joined Amnesty International. At youth group nights, over supper, the young people regularly write letters to help free political prisoners One person co-ordinates this by buying aerogrammes and photocopying the basic information and letter writing guides.

5. Another group joined Community Aid Abroad's 'Aware Program' in which they give $120 or more per year to the program and receive monthly information sheets about what projects the 'Awareness Program' is funding. They also support the Community Aid Abroad Walk Against Want each year.

6. Another group chose a project from the Uniting Church 'People in Partnership' projects, and after seeing videos and speakers on the project, raised money for it.

7. Members of a group became concerned about accommodation for young people. They decided on two strategies. They persuaded their church, in co-operation with another, to set up a house for homeless young people using assistance and advice from the State Community Service Division of their church.

And they started really encouraging people in their church to offer spare rooms in their houses for country kids coming to Melbourne.

There are lots of other possibilities. Perhaps you can add others.

Who else is involved in community and global issues?

The Uniting Church committee on social justice in your Synod can provide advice and resources about top priority social issues which should concern your group.

The Uniting Church committee for world mission in your Synod can provide advice and resources about issues affecting the lives of people in other parts of the world.

There are many agencies concerned with social issues and serving the community. In this country there is a strong government-run welfare system. The churches also provide care nurture and service.

Overseas aid and justice agencies like Community Aid Abroad, Action for World Development, World Vision, Amnesty International, Force Ten, support groups for the survivors of torture, are all involved in justice issues and are open to enquiries.

WORKSHEET 45: Justice in the time of Amos

Use this worksheet with your group to help you understand what God requires of humankind. Is it still the same today?

Amos speaks against injustice	What are today's parallels?
Chapter 1 verse 3 cruelty	
Chapter 1 verse 13 taking other people's land	
Chapter 2 verse 4 worship of false gods	
Chapter 2 verse 6 oppressing the poor	
Chapter 2 verse 7-8 sexual abuses	
Chapter 4 verse 4 ignoring justice	
Chapter 5 verse 14-15 what God requires	

How to work with young people. Copyright © 1991 The Joint Board of Christian Education

WORKSHEET 46: Interest or apathy

PURPOSE: To discover the current concerns of young people in the area of social issues.

HOW TO DO IT:

1. Put up a list of approximately ten social issues which are of concern in the community. Some possibilities:

    adequate aged pensions
    AIDS
    alcoholism
    capital punishment
    care of the mentally ill
    care for children with disabilities
    child abuse
    drug abuse
    homeless young people
    pollution
    pornography
    poverty
    prison reform
    quality of education
    racial discrimination
    road accidents
    sexual discrimination
    strikes
    unemployment benefits
    violence in the streets
    violence against women
    war

2. Give each person a blank sheet of paper, approximately A4 size. Ask them to draw a line down the left-hand margin. At the top of the line write, 'I feel very steamed up about...' At the bottom of the line write, 'I couldn't care less about...'

3. Ask members to list one of the social issues along the line according to their high interest (top) or apathy (bottom). Invite them to include other social issues which they feel to be important.

I feel very steamed up about...
    homeless young people
    care for children with disabilities
    sexual discrimination
    prison reform

I couldn't care less about...

Prepare on newsprint a continuum line for each of the social issues listed (plus spares for new issues raised). Record group feelings by putting ticks along the line:

Sexual discrimination

I feel very steamed up about...

I couldn't care less about...

This recording will show the importance that particular issues rate in the opinions of young people. The results may lead your program in particular directions.

- What can people do about the things they are steamed up about?
- Why do they not care about issues which harm the lives of many people?

YOU WILL NEED:

- A list of social issues, written on newsprint for all to see.
- Sheets of paper, pens or pencils, for individual recording of opinion.
- Newsprint for recording of group opinions on each issue
- Felt pen.

(Adapted From *Discovering the Needs and Interests of Young People* The Joint Board of Christian Education, Melbourne, used with permission.)

Chapter 13

Camping

Camping

Why should we have a camp?   177

How do we plan a good camp program?   177

What are some different styles of camping?   180

What do we do if there's an accident?   181

How do we prepare leaders for the camp?   182

WORKSHEET 47: Why should we have a camp?   187

WORKSHEET 48: Camp program planner   188

WORKSHEET 49: Parent's/guardian's declaration or camper's declaration if 18 years or over   189

WORKSHEET 50: Leader's self evaluation   191

WORKSHEET 51: Camp evaluation   192

WORKSHEET 52: Leadership skills booklet   193

WORKSHEET 53: Duty roster   197

WORKSHEET 54: Camp budget planning sheet   198

WORKSHEET 55: Finance sheet   199

Why should we have a camp?

Scene: Council of Elders meeting.

You have come to ask permission to hold a camp for young people. The last such camp was four years ago. Because of the unruly behaviour of campers, the Parish Council refused to let the group have another camp. Now the kids are keen to have another camp but you have to convince the minister and Parish Council that it's important.

List the main points you will make in your speech.

Camping has been a vital part of youth ministry for many years. Although camping styles have changed somewhat and new ones emerged, many of the basic values of youth camping have remained the same. What are some of the central contributions of camping to youth ministry?

Use WORKSHEET 47 to help you and your group decide what camping experiences can provide for you.

How do we plan a good camp program?

1. Who plans?
Appoint a camp planning group well in advance.

Meeting date: ....

Venue: ....

People: ....

....

....

....

....

....

2. Who comes?
Consider who will be attending the camp. Just your group? Invite another group? Invite friends? What leaders or camp parents?

3. Aims and objectives
Decide the camp aim – a general statement of what you want to achieve. This could include relationship building, skills training, service, spiritual growth.

Decide related objectives – specific statements as to how you will achieve these aims.

4. Style
Determine the style of the camp which best suits your aims. Brainstorm some possibilities first – day camp, tent camp, safari, canoe camp.

5. Choose date and venue
Identify suitable dates which would be convenient for potential campers. Avoid holiday times and exam times.

Make a list of possible venues in order of priority.

Points to keep in mind are –
– sleeping accommodation (total and room sizes)
– catered or self-catering

- toilet and washing facilities
- fresh water availability
- indoor meeting and recreational facilities
- outdoor recreational facilities
- worship setting
- offsite recreation options.

6. Theme

Choose a theme for your weekend which will help with advertising and building interest. This may relate to the studies, but also be reflected in other parts of the weekend.

If you wish to use an outside study leader, make a list of possible people and approach them.

7. Gather ideas and resources

Brainstorm ideas for studies, worship, recreation, community building based on your aims, objectives and theme.

Use any books or resources that seem relevant.

8. Plan the program

Decide on the basic camp program and time table, including meal times, studies, worship, free time. Use 'The camp program planner' (WORKSHEET 48 at the end of this chapter.)

Make decisions concerning:-
- leadership preparation prior to camp (see WORKSHEET 52)
- cooks
- equipment required
- transport
- arrival and registration procedure at camp
- music leadership, equipment, songbooks or overhead transparencies
- first aid equipment and person
- leaders' meetings during camp
- safety and accident procedures

- duty roster and clean-up (see WORKSHEET 53)
- budget and procedures for payments (see WORKSHEETS 54, 55)
- registration procedure prior to camp and acceptance letter (see WORKSHEET 49)
- camp rules and discipline.

9. Check

Check that the camp program planned is in accordance with the aims and objectives decided for the camp.

Confirm that you have approval from the appropriate church authorities to proceed with the camp.

10. Responsibility

Decide who will take overall responsibility for the camp. Allocate responsibility for each part of the camp program, that is, decide who will do the detailed planning of each session and activity.

(Use teams of groups, working with planning-team members, as leadership training.)

Don't forget to allocate responsibility for every part of the camp. Use 'Event planner' (WORKSHEET 26 at the end of chapter 7.)

11. Promotion

An attractive, informative camp form will build interest in the camp and attract new comers. Distribute the camp form at least 2 months prior to the camp. Use clip-art to make the form more attractive. Make sure you include the following information –
theme
registration deadline
dates
address for registration
place

contact person for enquiries
travel directions
who can come
starting and finishing times
name of sponsoring church and group
leaders' names
what to bring
something brief about the purpose of the camp
program highlights
speaker's name
alcohol restrictions
cost (who to make the cheque payable to).

Tear-off registration form should request details of –
name
date of birth
address
health insurance fund and number
home/work phone number
allergies/special medical
vegetarian/non vegetarian advice
emergency contact person and phone number
needs

Along with –

advice of payment enclosed

camper's signature (agreeing to abide by the camp rules)

indemnity or authorisation to participate signed by parent/guardian if camper is under 18 (see WORKSHEET 49 at the end of this chapter).

Personal contact and invitation is the most effective method of promotion.

12. Follow up

Overall camp leaders ensure that the required preparation is done by all people concerned.

13. Run the camp

Always take a box of items which might be useful e.g. newsprint, masking tape, felt pens, scissors, Frisbees, playing cards, tennis ball, table tennis equipment.

14. Evaluate

Have each camper fill in an evaluation sheet at the end of the camp. Hold a camp planning evaluation meeting to evaluate every aspect of the camp and its planning, and prepare a brief report to assist in planning the next camp (see WORKSHEETS 51, 52 at the end of this chapter).

Write thank-you letters to leaders and speaker and a follow-up letter to campers.

Visit any young people who have made significant faith commitments at camp.

Guidelines for effective youth camping

1. Plan properly.

2. Meet as leaders to prepare and pray for the camp.

3. Ensure that the camp is well publicised with an attractive camp form and personal invitation.

4. Visit the campsite before the weekend if you haven't been there before.

5. Make sure leaders are present at camp and the site is prepared well before campers arrive.

6. Spend time early on group-building activities even if you think people know each other. Use name tags.

7. Begin and close each day with worship/devotions.

8. Plan quiet times when campers can be alone with God and provide something printed to guide their reflection.

9. Make meal times fun with funny announcements, jokes, etc.

10. Use the 'small group' approach for studies and duties so campers get to know a few people quite well.

11. Balance studies and recreation time – don't have too much of either.

12. Allow at least 2 hours free time per day, but provide recreation options.

13. Ensure that duties are done well to maintain a high level of hygiene.

14. Have a first aid person available at all times and a pre-planned strategy if accidents happen.

15. Plan a few fun surprises at camp (not practical jokes).

16. Have a set lights out time and stick to it (11.00 p.m. is usually good for high school age).

17. Have clear rules and a consistent discipline procedure. Don't just let kids run riot.

18. Invite some caring adults to come as camp parents. If your minister is unable to attend the whole time, make sure he/she pays a visit.

19. Make your closing worship service a focus and highlight of the whole camp. Allow camper participation in the preparation and leadership of worship.

20. Give campers and leaders an evaluation sheet following the camp.

What are some different styles of camping?

There are many different types of camping – some require specialist skills and/or equipment, others do not. Here are a few.

Bike camp
Boat safari
Bus safari
Camp with young people who are disabled or disadvantaged
Canoeing camp
Country-city exchange
Day camp
Father/son; mother/daughter (or other combinations) camp
Fishing camp
Four wheel drive camp
Hiking camp
Horse riding camp
Leaders retreat/lock-in

YOUTH CAMPING STYLES							
STYLE	BASE	AIM	DURATION	RELIGIOUS CONTENT	PROGRAM	ORGANISATION	ACCOMMO-DATION
Parish youth group	Parish youth group	Group growth etc	Weekend (usually)	2 or 3 studies worship	Fairly structured	Leader & study leader	Varies
Adventure	Wide voluntary	Personal growth, group growth & awareness generally	One week (approx.)	By Christian presence – few structured moments	Fast moving activity orientated exciting	Considerable pre-planning & equipment necessary & high leadership component	Camp out
Safari	Parish or wider	Group growth etc	Day/weekend week or longer	Structured times & worship	Built about locations	Under 2 leaders usually	Camp out
Holiday camp	Parish or wider	Recreation & personal growth	Usually one week	Structured times & worship	Camper organised much free time	More than meets the eye	Usually residential
Work camp	Parish or wider	Specific & group growth	Weekend or longer	By Christian presence – few structured moments	Built around project	Considerable pre-organisation trained leaders	On site if possible
Outreach camp	Parish or wider	Evangelism & group growth	Weekend or week	Studies/worship & training for teams	Built about outreach little free time	Considerable pre-planning needs relationship to local church	On site if possible
Specific e.g. bike or horse riding 4 wheel drive music	Parish or wider	Skill & group growth	Weekend or longer	Devotional times & worship	Around skill	Considerable – leadership important	As appropriate
Inter generational	Parish or wider	Group growth	Weekend or longer	Studies (daily) & worship	Considerable free time	Leader & study leader	Usually residential
Highly structured	Wider	Group & personal growth	One week	Studies devotions worship	Highly organised	Considerable	Residential

Music camp
Mystery camp
Outreach camp
Overnight sleepover
Reef cruise
Residential campsite
   — beach
   — mountains

— lake
Sailing/water skiing camp
Snow camp
Spiritual retreat
Sporting camp
Study camp
Surfing camp
Survival camp

Tent camp (one site)
Train journey
Work camp
   Contact the Youth Ministry Office in your state to find out more about these different types of camping.

What do we do if there's an accident?

'Accidents will happen', they say, but they can usually be avoided. One should adopt the approach that prevention is better than having to mop up afterwards. How can camp leaders be prepared?

1. Make safety a high priority by taking the following steps seriously and stressing safety to leaders and campers.

2. Visit the campsite and talk to the managers. Be aware of any potentially dangerous places and establish clear 'out of bounds' areas. Communicate these clearly to campers.

3. Be aware of any activities which involve risk. These may include sport, swimming, night activities, hiking, climbing, abseiling, canoeing.
   Discuss these in detail as a whole leadership team, noting the risks involved.

4. Ensure that someone at camp has recent first aid training and that you have an up-to-date first aid kit.

5. Ensure that risk activities have experienced, sensible, and if necessary qualified instructors.

6. Discourage practical jokes at camp. Apart from being dangerous, these can be very harmful to a person's self-esteem.

7. Plan a sensible timetable. When people are tired they are always more at risk.

8. Establish a policy that campers can't leave the site without the permission of the camp leader.

9. When running activities, be alert for possible risks. Allow tired campers the option of sitting out. Don't allow too much rough activity or silly behaviour.

10. Ensure that campers have footwear when outdoors and wear sufficient sun-cover (hat, shirt, sunscreen).

If an accident occurs

1. Remain calm – a leader in a panic can't help anyone.
2. Ensure that the person is not in immediate danger.
3. Check immediately that pulse and breathing are OK.
4. Ensure that the person is in a comfortable position.
5. Notify another leader, preferably the Camp Director.

6. If the person can be moved, take them to the first aid facilities.
7. If the person cannot be moved, someone should stay with them until help comes.
8. If a doctor or ambulance is required, phone immediately. Note this should be done by the Camp Director.
9. If medical attention is required, parents must be notified as soon as possible.
10. Obtain the person's medical insurance information from the registration form.
11. A leader should accompany the injured person to the doctor or hospital.

Common safety problems and accidents

It's best to arrange for a qualified first aid person to train your leaders regarding accident prevention and first aid.

Minor accidents

PROBLEM	CAUSE	PREVENTION
cuts and scratches	glass or wire lying around, thorny bushes	prior site check, wear shoes
burns	scalding from hot water, fire	take seriously potential hazards
sunburn or sunstroke	over exposure to sun	wear hats, sunscreen, shirts
stings	nettles or thistles	learn to recognise them and warn campers
bites	ants, bees, wasps	choose activity areas carefully

More serious accidents		
Swimming: — check waterholes for depth and underwater obstructions — never allow swimming alone or unsupervised	— always have someone with lifesaving qualifications present Diving: — don't allow campers to dive into waterholes Fractured or broken limbs:	— warn campers of dangerous terrain and out-of-bounds areas — don't allow activities to get too rough — only suitably experienced leaders to set-up and supervise adventure equipment.

How do we prepare leaders for the camp?

Pre-camp leader training session

1. Team building

Session designed to start welding leaders into a team. Feedback, risk-taking, trust, acceptance, are issues that should be raised.

2. Housekeeping issues

Rosters, banking, dormitory allocation, leaders duties, bus captains, bus stop supervisors, etc. (where applicable).

3. Program work

Preparation of recreation – collective – skill section of the program. It is important to ensure leaders are competent in any skill areas they will be required to lead. If possible do some of all the creative activities and adventure activities so leaders have a clear understanding of what is involved and what (if any) dangers and safety procedures are involved. Creative work done by leaders here should be kept as teaching samples with the campers.

4. Project book and study materials

Go through in detail each of the studies to be conducted by leaders with their teams.

5. Working with children

Covering generally issues such as methods, discipline etc.

6. Campers

Allocation of leaders to teams and checking of special information or particular cases which leaders should be aware of in relation to particular children.

7. Expectations

Being sure what we expect from each other as leaders at each stage during the camp.

8. Leader information

During training days, make sure you have a completed camp leader application form from each leader. New leaders will have sent them in – have others fill one in so that you have a completed form from each leader. Give each leader a Leadership skills booklet (see WORKSHEET 52 at the end of this chapter).

Post camp evaluation

1. Team leader's evaluation

On the morning of the last day of camp give each leader a Leader evaluation form (WORKSHEET 50) and a Camp evaluation form (WORKSHEET 51) for them to fill out and bring completed to that night's leaders' meeting.

At the meeting leaders may like to share significant points from their forms or perhaps share an 'I learned' or 'I became aware' statement.

2. Camp leaders evaluation

After camp, the camp leader should write appropriate comments on the back of each leader's application form, staple it to that leader's evaluation form, and return it with the others to the Camp Convener.

3. Camp evaluation

After camp, the camp leader should also summarise the major points raised in the camp evaluation forms and add personal comments for the benefit of future planning.

Leading a small group

The leader does not lead or command in the popular sense, i.e. not always the focus of attention, the group-hero or strong person; neither does he/she manipulate or coerce the group to reach a personal hidden agenda.

The leader is not to know all the answers, or to keep the group happy by attempting to please everyone.

The leader should ensure that:
- the group is able to define its own goals and objectives;
- the group is not straying from the task or wasting time without realising it;
- participants are being accepted by each other, not put down;
- creative conflict is not being superficially brushed aside;
- members are listening to each other;
- quieter members are given reasonable opportunity to contribute;
- the group does not superficially reject the task (especially when the small group is part of a larger group);
- the group does not disrupt other groups;
- the group is not dominated or manipulated by one to two individuals;
- the group, or someone in it, is able to summarise the discussion/work done at appropriate times;
- as far as possible the physical setting is used to advantage so that it helps rather than hinders the group process.

NOTE: It is suggested that the leader should ensure that these things are done. This does not mean that the leader should do it all. If, for example, someone else is able to provide a useful summary then let them. Don't feel, as leader, that you have to do it. On the other hand, the leader must not opt out of responsibilities as a group participant; you should be willing to express your point of view (but not always be first to do so) rather than remaining mysterious and expecting everyone else to express an opinion.

Leading discussion

The art of the creative question or statement – to stimulate, clarify, interpret, define, identify, summarise.

Try to avoid asking questions which can be answered by 'yes' or 'no'. If the group is prodded for the 'right' answer, they will lose initiative and may become afraid to speak up. The questions you ask are not for information, but to direct thinking.

Discussion helpers:
'How do you feel about it?'
'Would you have acted differently?'
'What are some of the reasons why we act this way?'
'Tell us about it.'
'Why do you think it is so?'

Discussion stoppers:
'No, you are wrong.'
'That is not the right way to feel.'
'Why do you say a thing like that?'
'You should never say you hate anyone.'
'Oh, I'm sure that you don't really mean that.'
'Why is it bad to steal?'

Instead of saying 'No, that's not it at all', ask 'Are those the only two alternatives?' This will suggest to the group that there is another side of a more basic consideration to be aired. Remember that you're a real participant in the group and have a function in asking probing questions and contributing a much needed resource as background for the discussion. Your job is to help sense the depth of the question and to offer the church's experience when people seem ready for it.

Determining group level

Small groups operate at different 'levels' at different times.

The leader needs to be able to assess at what 'level' the group is, at any stage given time, and whether that level is appropriate.

1. Chit-chat: no serious conversation, no serious attempt to struggle with the problem/issue/task. People talk on the surface level not really meeting one another or taking one another seriously. (Sometimes other people are treated more as objects or things than people).

2. Academic discussion: talk as at an impersonal level. Subjects are kept 'out there' and discussed at an intellectual level (or are made fun of). Every problem is someone else's problem. (Sometimes other people are treated more as objects or things than people).

3. Personal discussion: participants are willing to express personal points of view rather than generalisations. There is acceptance of each other because of a sense of trust and honesty. While participants may not share fully, there is a freedom to share personal belief, doubts, joys, hopes without the fear of put downs or personal attack. ('I do not agree with that particular idea of yours, but I still accept you as a friend and welcome you as a group member'.)

Other people are accepted as equals – as persons of worth.

4. In-depth discussion: due to honesty, trust, warmth there are moments of deep meeting, moments of insight that arise out of intimate conversation and a deep level of acceptance and understanding. Because of the positive climate of this understanding group members are encouraged, and freed to risk new thoughts...to leap forward in faith rather than protect oneself. Other people are treated as precious companions.

NOTE: Each level is appropriate at different times. Groups will normally operate at levels 1 or 2 at the beginning of a meeting, or when members don't know each other well or perhaps as light relief during a 'heavy' discussion. The group leader should endeavour to encourage the group to operate at levels 3 and 4 for a significant amount of time. However, a good level of trust needs to be developed in the group first for this to happen.

Small group observer

Use this as a training activity with leaders. Divide into small groups and appoint a leader and an observer. Give the observer these instructions.

Sit opposite your partner and observe him/her carefully during the discussion.

Do not join in the conversation.

Take notes as to the participation of your partner in the group.

Did your partner ...
* Seem to be involved in the discussion (how much)?
* Express opinions?
* Express opinions clearly?

* Try to help others express their opinions more fully?
* Interrupt other people?
* Appear to opt out or switch off
* Change the subject at an inappropriate time?
* Try to draw others into the discussion?
* Help deepen the discussion on the subject?
* Crack a joke at an inappropriate time?
* Check that everyone understood what was going on (if necessary)?
* Dominate the discussion?
* Appear to be listening (verbally and non-verbally)?

The role of the team leader

Camp exists for the camper, yet it can be one of the greatest experiences of your life. It can broaden your vision, open new doors of service, give you insights into working with people, and contribute to your own spiritual growth and maturity in Christ. Though your own growth is not the primary function of camp, it is an important by-product of a good camp.

No matter what your background – college student, homemaker, businessperson, or pastor – the Holy Spirit wants to use you to accomplish God's purposes in the lives of your campers.

If this is your first experience in camp, you may be keenly aware of how your new situation contrasts with the business world. Instead of a 'What can I get out of this?' attitude, team leaders need to ask, 'How much can I give of myself?'

The team leader and the director

The team leader has a responsibility to the director in several respects:

a) Loyalty. Except on a matter of a high principle, they must be loyal to the policies and rulings of the director.

b) Openness. They should be willing to honestly say what they think, and if necessary, willing to be rebuked or taught where they are in error or ignorance

c) Willingness to do small jobs. There is no privileged class on a camp team. There are lots of things that have to be done by every team member.

d) Providing feedback. They should keep the director informed about what is going on at the group level – plans, difficulties, equipment requirements or breakages, and especially the morale of the campers. They have a very important role here in the evaluation of the impact of the studies and teaching program on the campers.

The team leader and other leaders

The same kinds of things apply to the leader's relationship with other leaders. They must be willing to accept majority decisions and to back up other leaders in implementing them.

Their personal relationships with the rest of the team are very important. Firstly, they must be tolerant – of their personal idiosyncrasies, their denominational and cultural differences. Secondly, they must avoid exclusive relationships with another leader intruding on the sense of community and caring of the team as a whole. Two heads together in a corner suggest secrets being shared, but hidden from the rest of the team. Good friends who lead on camps together must be sensitive to the hard feelings that they may cause, however unjustified they may be.

The team leader and the camp as a whole

There are temptations for the team leader to become so involved with the interests of his/her own team and become careless of the welfare of the camp as a whole. Every leader must play a part in adequate pre-camp preparation, practical jobs within the program, duties (where good leadership can really make camp spirit) and watchfulness over camper safety and equipment care. It is not sufficient for a leader to turn a blind eye to Daryl stuffing a paint brush in Jennifer's ear because Daryl is in Mac's team.

The team leader and the team

Team leaders must look after the camper's welfare. This includes the camper's:

a) Health. They should know whether their campers are feeling well, or homesick, or tired.

b) Comfort. They should know whether their campers are warm enough at night, getting enough to eat and have some way of getting home afterwards.

c) Safety. They should know where their campers are, as far as practicable. They should prevent dangerous pranks in their own living area and make sure their campers know the rules and regulations concerning water safety, fires, leaving grounds etc.

d) Behaviour. Good discipline can only be maintained if the team leader assists with a positive effort at the team level.

e) Spiritual welfare. The team leader should be alert to opportunities that arise naturally, to answer questions, or talk personally with the camper. The good team leader does not and should not coerce a camper, by using a personal relationship as a lever.

f) Continuing contact. If camp is often a time of beginnings – changes of attitude, a new desire to live differently, perhaps a first commitment to Christ or a desire to stay in contact with a group of Christians – then it is our responsibility to help the camper continue this beginning into everyday life.

With respect to these last two points, it is important to remember that some camper will relate more readily to the leader of another team than to their own team leader. You can't expect relationships to automatically blossom in the teams you have, whether the teams were chosen by you, the campers or both. Therefore you can't make rigid rules about the team leader's spiritual responsibility for each member of his/her group. What we can say is that team leaders should make every effort to ensure that someone has a continuing contact with each of their group, or at least keeps the lines of communication open with each of their campers. Where a camper has sought counsel from a particular leader, then that leader is the obvious person to continue the contact.

WORKSHEET 47: Why should we have a camp?

Use the boxes to do two things.

1. Rank which of these you see as most important on a scale of 1 to 10 (1 = most important).

2. Rank which of these your group would see as most important.

☐ ☐ Camping provides a change from our normal routine. By stepping back and reflecting on our lives we have the opportunity for significant growth by developing new patterns of behaviour.

☐ ☐ Camping is an experience of Christian community.
At camp we experience deepening of relationships, and the joys and struggles which accompany that growth.

☐ ☐ Camping provides outdoor experiences.
At many camps we have time to appreciate the beauty of God's creation.

☐ ☐ Camping is a wholistic environment.
Because we share together in meals, learning, duties, relaxation and worship, we may learn about the rhythms of a more wholistic lifestyle.

☐ ☐ Camping provides opportunity for encounter with God.
Camps give special times for reflection, worship, sharing, and solitude through which we may experience a deeper sense of God's presence and purpose for our lives.

☐ ☐ Camps give opportunity for physical recreation.
Camp activities allow young people to have fun, develop new skills, enjoy friendships and just let off steam.

☐ ☐ Camps provide a sense of adventure. Camp programs can provide opportunities for challenge, exploration, and using initiative. Through decision-making in difficult situations, young people gain a sense of achievement and self confidence.

☐ ☐ Camping provides opportunity for relaxation. People need rest as part of their recreation. Free time, time to unwind and adequate sleep are part of the wholistic camping experience.

☐ ☐ Camping provides opportunity for Christian education. While camps are great fun, they should also provide opportunity for Christian nurture through spoken input, discussion, learning activities and media. Many young people come to significant faith commitment through camps.

☐ ☐ Camping provides opportunities for corporate worship. Camp worship experiences may be especially meaningful because of the relaxed environment, shared planning and participation, and the chance to focus the whole camp on God.

WORKSHEET 48: Camp program planner

DAY	DAY	DAY	DAY	DAY	DAY
	Wake up	Wake up			
	Breakfast	Breakfast			
	Morning Tea	Morning Tea			
	Lunch	Lunch			
	Afternoon Tea	Afternoon Tea			
	Tea				
Arrive					
Bed	Bed				

WORKSHEET 49: Parents/guardians declaration or camper's declaration if 18 years or over

I the undersigned am willing that I/my child .... should participate in the above camp being held between / / and / / .

I understand that the nature of the activities at the camp will include, but may not be limited to hiking, swimming, games, dormitory accommodation, communal eating, dancing, and that risks may arise during these activities.

I HEREBY AUTHORISE the leader in charge of the camp or the particular activity in which I am/my child is involved to consent, where it is impracticable to communicate with me/to my child receiving such medical or surgical treatment as the leader in charge may deem necessary at any time during the trip. I further authorise the use of an ambulance and/or anaesthetic by a qualified medical practitioner if in his/her judgment it is necessary. I accept responsibility for payment of all expenses associated with such treatment.

FOR PARENTS/GUARDIANS ONLY:

I understand that every effort will be made by the leader firstly to contact me in the event of such illness or accident.

This is/is not the first time my child has been away from home without the company of a parent/guardian.

I confirm that the particulars given on the accompanying confidential medical report form are correct.

EVERYONE MUST SIGN THE FOLLOWING:

DATED: This .... day of .... 19............................

SIGNED: ....

CONFIDENTIAL MEDICAL REPORT

The information given below is requested to assist in case of any illness or accident. The information will be held in confidence and this form will be destroyed after the camp.

1. Are you/is your child presently taking tablets and/or medicine? YES/NO
If yes please state the name of the medication, dosage, etc.

....

***PLEASE NOTE that the leader in charge is authorised to require that all medicines for children under 18 years are handed to him/her at the commencement of the camp with your child's name and dosage and time of taking marked clearly on the label. Children under 18 years are not permitted to be in possession of any medicine during the camp.

2. Child's/your name: ....

Child's date of birth: ....

Parent's/guardian's full name: ....

Address: ....

....

EMERGENCY PHONE NO:

Business: .... Home..

Name and address of family doctor: ....

....

Medicare No.: ....

Medical/hospital Insurance Fund: ....

Contribution Number: ....

3. ALLERGIC TO:

☐ Penicillin

☐ Any foods ....

☐ Others ....

☐ Any special care? ....

☐ Last tetanus immunisation: ....

☐ If over 5 years since immunisation, please tick if booster is to be arranged by you/parents.

Please tick if you/your child suffers from any of the following:

☐ Dizzy spells   ☐ asthma

☐ fits of any type   ☐ sleep walking

☐ heart condition   ☐ migraines

☐ blackouts   ☐ travel sickness

☐ other ....

Signed .... Date / /

WORKSHEET 50: Leader evaluation

CAMP   PLACE   DATE

....

(To be completed by all leaders at the final leaders' meeting and returned to the camp leader)

1. How would you rate your performance as a leader

_____

lousy   poor   fair   good   excellent

2. List 2 or 3 of your main personal learnings:

....

....

....

3. What weaknesses did you become aware of in your leadership?

....

....

....

4. What extra training and preparation do you feel you need to become more effective?

....

....

....

5. What will be the effect of this weekend's experience on your back-home situation?

....

....

....

You are invited to sign this sheet

....

WORKSHEET 51: Camp evaluation

CAMP   PLACE   DATE

....

(To be completed by all leaders at the final leaders' meeting and returned to the camp leader)

1. How would you rate the camp?

_____

lousy   poor   fair   good   excellent

2. What were the main strengths?

....

....

....

3. What were the main weaknesses?

....

....

....

4. Would you like to comment on –

(a) Team relationships

(b) Studies ....

(c) Worship ....

(d) Program ....

(e) Food ....

(f) Venue...

(g) Camp organisation ....

                                                                                          Name

                                        ....

WORKSHEET 52: Leadership skills booklet

The following can be made up into a booklet to assist you to develop your leadership skills as a result of your involvement in the camp.

* SECTION ONE is for completion prior to the camp.

* SECTION TWO is for work during the camp. (Do one part each day.)

* SECTION THREE is to help you draw together the experience and identify your growth points before you leave camp.

* Hand your Journal to the Chaplain or Director and if you can, find time to talk with them at the same time. The Journal will be returned to you after the camp.

LEADER SELF EVALUATION/DEVELOPMENT JOURNAL

CAMP ....

LEADER'S NAME ....

ADDRESS..

....

PHONE ....

SECTION ONE

Please complete PRIOR to camp.

* These are the gifts/skills/talents that I bring to camp –

....

....

....

....

....

* My weaknesses/areas of insecurity are –

....

....

....

....

....

* Specific things I want to achieve during this week –

....

....

....

....

....

....

....

....

SECTION TWO

Complete one part each day during camp.

DAY 1 My first impression of my group –

....

In my relationship with my group I want to work on –

....

....

DAY 2 Highlights of today were –

....

....

I could have contributed more today if I had –

....

DAY 3 A camper I want to get to know better tomorrow is ....
because –

....

I am going to do this by –

....

DAY 4 Tonight, focus on the spiritual dimensions of camp. Recall contributions to spiritual growth of camper/s that you have made so far –

....

....

Make some specific plans for tomorrow. Name the camper/s and be specific about what you want to talk about with them.

....

....

DAY 5 What would you say is your group's impression of you after the camp together?

....

How well have you achieved your goals set last night and the night before?

....

SECTION THREE

Complete this section BEFORE LEAVING THE CAMPSITE and hand to Chaplain or Director.

A. EVALUATING THE CAMP

Strengths/highlights –

....

Weaknesses/low spots –

....

Suggestions –

....

....

B. EVALUATE YOURSELF

List 2 or 3 of your personal learnings or areas of growth.

....

....

Your major weakness?

....

What changes will those back home see in you?

....

How will you change your operation in your family/ group/ church/ Sunday school etc.?

....

What specific ideas, games, studies, methods used at camp will I be able to use in my local church? (Include when and details of the group.)

....

Other comments:

....

....

Would you like to comment on the usefulness of this Journal?

....

WORKSHEET 53: Duty roster

DAY:... DATE:..

Please put your name on the roster below to be available once for one of today's camp duties. It is important that we have some guys and girls on each duty. We should finish with a name against each of the numbers *circled* below.

Breakfast Preparation
- 1. .... 4. ....
- 2. .... 5. ....
- 3. .... 6. ....

Breakfast Cleanup
- 1. .... 4. ....
- 2. .... 5. ....
- 3. .... 6. ....

Lunch Preparation
- 1. .... 4. ....
- 2. .... 5. ....
- 3. .... 6. ....

Lunch Cleanup
- 1. .... 4. ....
- 2. .... 5. ....
- 3. .... 6. ....

Dinner Preparation
- 1. .... 4. ....
- 2. .... 5. ....
- 3. .... 6. ....

Dinner Cleanup
- 1. .... 4. ....
- 2. .... 5. ....
- 3. .... 6. ....

Supper Preparation
- 1. .... 4. ....
- 2. .... 5. ....
- 3. .... 6. ....

Supper Cleanup
- 1. .... 4. ....
- 2. .... 5. ....
- 3. .... 6. ....

Wash Teatowels
- 1. .... 4. ....
- 2. .... 5. ....
- 3. .... 6. ....

Other
- 1. .... 4. ....
- 2. .... 5. ....
- 3. .... 6. ....

WORKSHEET 54: Camp budget planning sheet

CAMP ATTENDANCE

(i)   Estimated no. of campers   = ...

(ii)   Estimated no. of leaders   = ...

(iii)   Estimated no. of extras (children)   = ...

                                            TOTAL   = _____ A.

          LESS no. of non-paying campers   = ...

        TOTAL no. of paying campers/leaders   = _____ B.

EXPENSES   **TOTAL**

1. Variable (dependant on no. of campers)

(i)   Campsite cost per night x No. of campers (A.)

            .... x ....   = $ ....

(ii)   No. of meals x Cost per meal x No. of campers

         Breakfast .... x .... x = $ ....

         Lunch   .... x .... x = $ ....

         Dinner   .... x .... x = $ ....

         Supper   .... x .... x = $ ....

         Teas   .... x .... x = $ ....

         (Morning/

         Afternoon)   Meals total   = $ _____   ....

(iii)   Activities   = $ ....

(iv)   Other .... = $ ....

                         TOTAL VARIABLE COST = $ _____ C.

B. Fixed (regardless of no. of campers)

(i)   Transport (bus hire)   = $ ....

(ii)   Printing camp form   = $ ....

(iii)   Printing study booklet   = $ ....

(iv)   Equipment hire: ....   = $ ....

                        ....   = $ ....

                        ....   = $ ....

(v)   Speaker's honorarium   = $ ....

(vi)   Other .... = $ ....

                             TOTAL FIXED COST = $ _____ D.

SUMMARY (Camp Fee)

                     TOTAL VARIABLE COSTS (C.) = $ ....

                        TOTAL FIXED COSTS (D.) = $ ....

                                PROFIT MARGIN = $ ....

                          TOTAL CAMP COST = $ _____ E.

COST PER PAYING CAMPER (E.) .... divided by (B.) .... = $ _____

WORKSHEET 55: Finance sheet

CAMP OR ACTIVITY ....

NAME OF PERSON ACCEPTING RESPONSIBILITY ....

PAYMENTS MADE BY YOU FROM CASH ADVANCED:

Bought from	Items bought (attach any receipts)	Food	Art & craft items	Other items

● Please NO NOT refund any fees (or part of fees) by cash

TOTAL OF AMOUNTS PAID $ .... : ....

TOTAL OF CASH RECEIVED $ .... : ....

CASH RETURNED WITH THIS SHEET $ .... : ....
OR
CASH DUE TO YOU $ .... : ....

RECOMMENDED READING

Reaching Youth Today: Heirs to the Whirlwind. Barbara Hargrove and Stephen Jones. Judson Press, Valley Forge, 1982.

Youth World and Church. Sara Little. John Knox Press, Richmond, 1968.

Christian Youth Work. Mark Ashton. Kingsway, Sussex, 1986.

Inside Out. Michael Eastman. Falcon, London, 1976.

Building an Effective Youth Ministry. Glen E. Ludwig. Abingdon Press, Nashville, 1979.

Portrait of Youth Ministry. Maria Harris. Paulist Press, New York, 1981.

Youth and the Community of Disciples. David Ng. Judson Press, Valley Forge, 1984.

Catching the Rainbow. J. David Stone. Abingdon Press, Nashville, 1981.

Youth Ministry. Ginny Ward Holderness. John Knox Press, Atlanta, 1980.

Total Youth Ministry. Maria Edwards, RSM. St.Marys, Minnesota.

Celebration of Discipline. Richard Foster. Hodder & Stoughton, London, 1980.

Youth Ministry: Making and Shaping Disciples. Jeffrey D. Jones. Judson Press, Valley Forge, 1976.

Youth Ministry – Thinking Big with Small Groups. Carolyn Brown. Abingdon Press, Nashville, 1984.

Youth Ministry Encyclopedia. Lyman Coleman. Serendipity/JBCE, 1984.

12-14 Year Olds in the Church. Mary-Ruth Marshall. JBCE, Melbourne, 1982.

Recruitment and Training. Grant Nichol, UCA Department of Field Services, Melbourne.

Small, Rural and Isolated Youth Groups. Geraldine Anderson. JBCE, Melbourne, 1987.

Getting Involved: 15-17 year olds in the church. Geraldine Anderson. JBCE, Melbourne, 1987.

Young People and Your Church. Ed. Heather McMinn. JBCE, Melbourne, 1989

Young People and Your Church – Action Manual. Ed. Heather McMinn, Uniting Church Press, Melbourne, 1989.

Growing Christians in Small Groups. John Mallison. Anzea/JBCE, 1989.